Suite Success

Suite Success

The Psychologist from
The Apprentice Reveals
What It Really Takes to Excel—
in the Boardroom and in Life

Liza Siegel, Ph.D.

AMACOM AMERICAN MANAGEMENT ASSOCIATION

New York • Atlanta • Brussels • Chicago • Mexico City • San Francisco
Shanghai • Tokyo • Toronto • Washington, D.C.

Special discounts on bulk quantities of AMACOM books are available to corporations, professional associations, and other organizations. For details, contact Special Sales Department, AMACOM, a division of American Management Association, 1601 Broadway, New York, NY 10019.
Tel.: 212-903-8316. Fax: 212-903-8083.
Website: www.amacombooks.org

Library of Congress Cataloging-in-Publication Data

Siegel, Liza, 1957-
    Suite success : the psychologist from The Apprentice reveals what it really takes to excel—in the boardroom and in life / Liza Siegel.
        p. cm.
    Includes bibliographical references and index.
    ISBN-10: 0-8144-7360-1 (hardcover)
    ISBN-13: 978-0-8144-7360-3
    1. Success in business—Psychological aspects. 2. Creative ability in business. 3. Attitude (Psychology) 4. Optimism. 5. Self-confidence. I. Title.

HF5386.S448 2006
650.1—dc22   *2006002738*

Printing number

10 9 8 7 6 5 4 3 2 1

Contents

Foreword

WHEN DR. LIZA SIEGEL first walked into my office in Santa Monica for her interview, I had my fingers crossed that we had finally found our location psychologist. We were scheduled to begin filming *Survivor III* in Africa about five months later, and we were having trouble finding someone with just the right qualifications who would also be low-maintenance enough to tolerate the rugged conditions of location work.

Before we began the first *Survivor* we had hired Dr. Richard Levak, a leading expert in personality testing, to help us screen people during the casting process. Richard had proved to be an invaluable resource at helping us predict how people would fare under harsh conditions and social competition. Now all we needed to make it work was a psychologist who could help during the casting process and who would also be available on location after people were "voted off the island."

Richard, who is quite good at predicting behavior, felt that Liza could do the job. She seemed warm and personable, and definitely had the right credentials, but there was no way to determine how she would do in the elements, especially considering that she wore a powder-blue suit and was well-coiffed and manicured during the interview that first day. We decided to give her a chance, and the first time I saw her on location, knee-deep in dust with a ponytail and no makeup, I was relieved that she fit right in. I am very glad that we took that chance, because five years later Liza is the first person I turn to when it comes to looking after the well-being of the contestants I send onto my reality shows.

Something that all of my shows have in common is an element of people's enduring an extreme challenge. I know first-hand how mentally and emotionally exhausting an endurance challenge can be. Nine years before *Survivor*, I happened upon an article in that day's *Los Angeles Times* about the adventure race, the Raid Gauloises. Although I had created a successful marketing business, something was missing in my life and that article spoke to me about what I needed to do next. I made up my mind to create my own expedition-length race in the United States and called it the Eco-Challenge.

I also decided that it wouldn't do to just sit back and produce such an adventure without knowing what it felt like to actually compete, so I signed up for the next Raid Gauloises, which would take place in the Arab country of Oman. During that race the environmental and physical challenges were staggering, and my team weathered fatigue, storms, injuries, and getting lost. The darkest moment came when one of our team members did the unthinkable: he quit, leaving us one person short of the requirement to finish with a full team! Through all of this I experienced every human emotion at some point in the race, ranging from despair and rage to joy and euphoria.

I am proud that I have been through such a raw experience, but I also know that this is not to be taken lightly. I have always wanted to make sure that the individuals in all of my reality shows are well supported afterward. Over the course of all of the past seasons of *The Apprentice*, Liza has been the one who the contestants turn to for support after they are fired. It may seem unnecessary, and may sound uncharacteristically soft for an adventurer and risk-taker like me, but I know that the shows I create tap into a very basic part of the psyche, for both the viewer and the participant. That is part of what makes those shows so compelling to watch, but I don't want to put people at risk for the sake of good television.

Both *The Apprentice* and *Survivor* deal with the painful emotions that all humans experience when they are excluded from something, whether they are voted off as in the case of *Survivor* or fired as on *The Apprentice*. In primitive times, if you were excluded from the tribe, it would mean certain death, and both shows evoke that same feeling of being "killed," whether it is by having your torch snuffed out by Jeff Probst or having the desk slammed and hearing the words "You're Fired" from Donald Trump.

That emotional hook is what makes the audience relate to the shows, but the characters who have just been "killed" aren't actors and they genuinely experience those emotions in the moment. Having Liza there as someone they can talk to afterward gives them an opportunity to put into place what they just went through, both the highs and the lows. Many contestants who have been though that level of challenge and competition are able to use what they have learned about themselves to make positive changes in their lives, and Liza is there to help them make sense of it all.

Getting fired on national television is not an easy thing, nor is surviving on an island without food or shelter for six weeks. The shows that interest me are those that push people to their limits by placing them in extreme conditions. Obviously we don't want anyone getting hurt, so we select only those individuals who are hardy enough to handle such extreme conditions. What Liza and I have observed in this select group of competitors is that their attitude and mental states are central to their high levels of achievement, both on the show and in their personal lives. Liza has been on the sidelines, watching, observing, and making sense of all of these high-energy, Type A, optimistic, and outgoing personalities for the past five years. During that time she has compiled some fascinating information about what fuels success. Just as I discovered in that first Raid Gauloises in Oman, it is qualities like optimism, staying positive, and self-control that push you forward when the challenges seem insurmountable.

I have always believed that my career has been strengthened by building success out of chaos. With every setback I steeled my reserves; with the important lessons I learned from my mistakes, I have always, always moved forward. Many people wonder how I can successfully run multiple series at any given time, and aside from surrounding myself with great people, I believe that moving forward and not dwelling on the past gives me the freedom and the energy to juggle many projects. I don't believe in defeat and I am always excited about the future. This is the same attitude that we find in the candidates for *The Apprentice*.

With colorful examples from the show, Liza's book outlines the importance of positive qualities like resilience and optimism, in determining the difference between success and failure. Before you jump to any conclusions, "success" isn't confined to just the final person who is selected to be the Apprentice. Anyone who is adventurous, talented, and enthusiastic enough to make it through the challenging process of competing on *The Apprentice* is an excellent example of a driven Type A personality. The person's ultimate placement in the show is irrelevant. As I have learned over the past twenty years, if you're not failing, you're not taking enough chances.

The talented and dynamic people who apply to my shows are the ones who are out there taking chances every day. Does that mean that they are successful in the "real" business world? I guess that would depend on how you measure success, but since casting the first *Apprentice* I have met hundreds of self-made entrepreneurs who are passionate about what they do and who are earning more in their early twenties than the average forty-year-old in Corporate America. What sets them apart is what Liza talks about in this book. They are driven and ambitious, and they don't take no for an answer. When they get fired, it hurts, but what they do next is the real lesson in business because they are not quitters, and they quickly bounce back. What allows them to bounce back is an optimistic outlook.

Many books have been written about having a positive attitude, but Liza's book makes the qualities of optimism and resilience quite concrete, with great examples from the show. As she is able to do when she works with the contestants, she turns her knowledge of human behavior and psychology into something that is genuinely helpful.

On many occasions, and in various locations around the globe, Liza and I have discussed the amazing tenacity and human spirit that are revealed when our contestants push themselves to new limits. It is my hope that this book will leave you with a sense that you too can survive any endurance challenge, whether it is waged in the elements or in the corporate jungle.

Mark Burnett
Executive Producer of *The Apprentice* and *Survivor*

Acknowledgments

SEVERAL YEARS AGO I had the good fortune to meet Dr. Richard Levak, my mentor, my colleague, and my good friend. I owe him special thanks because much of what is contained in this book reflects all that he has taught me about how to conceptualize "personality."

Mark Burnett has always made time to hear my thoughts and from our very first meeting has encouraged me to write a book. Kevin Harris and Jay Beinstock have shared that encouraging spirit and have been extremely helpful even though they had many other demands on their time.

The coordinators who travel to location were very sweet and protective of my time so that I could finish this project. For proofreading, support, and protective services, I want to thank *all* of the coordinators from the past seasons and especially: Lauren Brock, Libby Hollingsworth, Jen and Scott Salyers, Erin Connolly, Aaron Roos, Jill Goslicky, Ronnie Stephenson, and Caitlin Moore. Thanks also to David Eilenberg for his creative input for the title to this book and to Kevin Gilbert for the contestant photographs.

Audrey Nieh holds a special place in my heart. She is the fastest typist on the planet and one of the smartest and most creative people I know.

Grateful acknowledgment is made to Sonja Lyubomirsky and Springer Press for permission to reprint the Subjective Happiness Scale. Thanks also to my book agent, Bill Gladstone, for patiently keeping the faith and seeing this project through to completion.

The following individuals have graciously granted permission to be included in this book: Amy Henry, Bill Rancic, Bowie Hogg, David Gould, Jessie Conners, Katrina Campins, Kwame Jackson, Nick Warnock, Omarosa Manigault Stallworth, Sam Solovey, Troy McClain, Andy Litinsky, Chris Russo, Kelly Perdew, Pamela Day, Raj Bhakta, Bren Olswanger, Brian McDowell, Danny Kastner, John Gafford, and Tana Goertz.

The Editor in Chief, my Mom, has edited everything I have written from grade school to present. She always encouraged my love of writing and my love of learning. Thanks also to Dr. Laura Goldin and Dr. Laurel Lippert for editing from the psychologist's perspective.

Tony, my husband, possesses every quality mentioned in this book. He has the confidence and the optimism to tackle any project, and I believe with all my heart that there isn't anything he can't do.

Penni Lane Clifton, my daughter, was the inspiration for the sections in this book about relationships and charisma: she *is* that person who gravitates to the leadership role. As I have watched her over the years, her quick wit, appealing personality, and ability to form relationships have been a source of delight and pride. Through all of our adventures, Penni will always be my companion and kindred spirit.

Suite Success

How I Stumbled on Optimism in Reality Television

WHEN MARK BURNETT first suggested that I write a book, it was during my initial job interview to be a consulting psychologist on the third season of *Survivor*. There were two producers in the room and Mark was being the "good cop." The other producer was telling me that he hated psychologists, that they were all weird, and that I'd better not screw up. Mark, on the other hand, told me that it was a great job and best of all, I could research and write a book. Two seasons later, Mark brought up the book idea again. There was a perfect lab experiment going on every season, and the stories about human behavior were endless.

Trying to fall asleep that night was difficult: we were on location on a remote island, it was hot and stuffy, and my bed was full of sand, which made my bug bites itch even more than usual. All night the old social psychology experiments about altruism, group cohesion, and conditioning played through my head. Yes, we really had it all happening in the course of any given season.

I am not the type of person to act quickly. I need a nice, long time to ponder an issue and look at it from every angle. My need to be slow and methodical is exactly why I am not the entrepreneurial type, so it is ironic that by the time I made up my mind about what I wanted to write about, I was working on *The Apprentice*! It took me a while to zero in on one topic that interested me most, but I finally realized that I was most excited about the huge lesson I had learned when I interviewed applicants as part of the casting process.

When prospective candidates relate their family histories, they almost always give them a positive spin, even when there were hardships along the way. This is decidedly different from the typical clinical interview in most outpatient clinics where I had worked. These applicants don't focus on what they didn't have or what had been hurtful growing up. The positive slant they give to their childhood spills over into their current success and even predicts their successes on the show. This could have been just coincidence, but it also happens that positive psychology, a relatively young branch of psychology, is accumulating studies about the impact that optimism and a positive outlook have on personal and professional success. I finally had a topic for my book!

An optimistic outlook is something that I also saw in Mark Burnett and Donald Trump; indeed, it seems to be a catalyst for the drive that pushes such business titans constantly forward. Although the business world had never interested me much in college, the excitement and enthusiasm that *The Apprentice* candidates had for business, real estate, and even finance were contagious and showed me that the thrill of the deal is much more motivating than simply making money. As I began to think about how optimism influences this group of candidates in the world of business, I also realized that it is a shaping force in my own ability to overcome adversity.

While the candidates for the show are on the extreme end of optimism, I am a little further to the middle, but very rarely have I been pessimistic. Some would say I am naively positive; I've had friends tease me that I live in "Candyland" when it comes to trusting people and seeing their best side. I've always seen the best in people, and I have always been interested in what makes them tick.

I guess my daughter, Penni, was my first study in temperament. I can honestly say that she was born a realist, slightly cautious yet always optimistic about the big picture. She is outgoing and friendly, extremely loyal to her circle of friends. So we were quite a pair growing up together. I had just turned eighteen years old when I had Penni, and it was my naivete that fooled me into thinking that everything would be just fine—but it always was! I went back to college when she was in the first grade, and I didn't stop to question whether it would be too difficult to attend classes as a single parent. I just signed up for the courses I wanted, mostly psychology, and even took an extra class every semester so that I could finish early.

The difference that a positive outlook has made on my life has kept me from becoming another statistic of teenage pregnancy. Having my daughter turned out to be the biggest blessing of my life. Together we went through both undergraduate and graduate school, as well as Officer Training School in the U.S. Air Force. Although optimistic about the big picture, I sometimes fret over the details. I learned a lot from the extreme examples on *The Apprentice*. I have seen their attitude in action, especially how it plays out in the world of business and leadership. What the applicants have shown me is that there is a way to be determinedly upbeat even when all the signs indicate otherwise.

Although I was suspicious at first about the positive pictures they paint, I couldn't ignore the data. The fact was that these people have a natural exuberance and optimistic outlook that even shows up in their personality tests. They rarely get depressed or anxious, have a high level of energy, and are very sociable and outgoing. This translates to personal and professional success. As a group, they have a high average income, even though they are typically in their early twenties! Their personal lives are quite enviable as well, and most have very happy relationships and many close friends.

Since working on *The Apprentice,* I've noted that the positive virtues and personality qualities that seem to be most closely related to leadership are optimism, creativity, resilience, a balance between self-control and passion, emotional awareness, and sociability. These positive personality characteristics flesh out what is meant in leadership schools about having vision, or resolve, or charisma.

Vision is an elusive term, but when you think about it in regard to having an optimistic outlook and the ability to see things creatively, it makes it easier to understand and apply. The *resolve* of a leader involves being resilient—bouncing back from inevitable setbacks—as well as applying elbow grease to a job in order to achieve results. This sometimes means having the self-control to put off the pleasures of the moment in order to reach a long-term gain. And a good leader is thought to have *charisma* when he inspires people to follow his suggestions. A lot of things go into making someone charismatic, from the way he looks to his persuasive ability, but the charm of *The Apprentice* candidates relates to their emotional awareness and ability to be warm and friendly. They are extroverted and sociable folks who are hard to resist. Not only are they successful, they are a lot of fun to be around!

Although I spend quite a bit of personal time with many candidates, I have confined my examples in this book to those in segments that aired on television or to biographical facts published elsewhere, to respect the private nature of their conversations with me. Any general examples given are about conglomerates of contestant characteristics and do not represent one person. In the few instances where I talk about applicants' reactions after they were fired, the individuals have given their explicit consent to what has been written. Each of the contestants mentioned consented to and approved the material in this book. Additionally, there wasn't enough time to mention every candidate from every show, but each one of them could have been an example of the positive qualities that lead to success.

Chapters 2 through 7 are devoted to each of the six personal qualities that lead to success in business. There are suggestions at the end of each chapter for improving abilities in these areas. Additionally, Chapter 1 offers an overview of the positive emotions and personal qualities and the place they have in the business world.

This book can show you how positive emotions can lead to better leadership. Behavioral science has made great strides in untangling the complicated picture of a healthy work environment and a successful career. The pages ahead will help you apply that knowledge and will give you tools to infuse positive qualities into your own leadership style.

The Power of Staying Positive

How we choose what we do, and how we approach it, will determine whether the sum of our days adds up to a formless blur or to something resembling a work of art.

—MIHALY CSIKSZENTMIHALYI, professor of psychology and management at the Peter Drucker School of Business at Claremont University and author of *Finding Flow* and other books on happiness and creativity

IT IS NO SECRET that we spend a lion's share of our time and energy on work. For some, work is a means to an end—a way to bring home a paycheck—but for most of us, work is where we look to find happiness and give meaning to life. So it's natural that we would want to learn as much as possible about how to make our work more satisfying.

Today's business leaders seek more guidance in the form of

training, seminars, business books, and coaching than ever before. Despite all of the information available, and although many wear the role of leadership with a tailored good fit, there are still those who lag behind, slightly disheveled and pulling at the seams. Regardless of our position in business, we have a natural curiosity about what it takes to excel. Theories abound, but one of the most basic questions involves the old "nature versus nurture" debate. Obviously, some people are naturally gifted with innate leadership ability, but higher education certainly also contributes its fair share to the talent.

When the producers of the first *Apprentice*—a reality television show about competing for an apprenticeship with Donald Trump—began constructing a story line, they wanted to know just that: Who would be the winner? Which applicant would have what it takes to stand out in a crowd—the Harvard MBA or the scrapper with natural-born "street smarts"? What creates an excellent leader? Is leadership an inborn quality, is it acquired through education and training, or is it both?

> **What creates an excellent leader? Is leadership an inborn quality, is it acquired through education and training, or is it both?**

As the first season unfolded, the person with the highest level of education was the first person fired, and the least educated of the bunch made it to the final five. In this case, art imitated life and reality television reflected some real facts about good leadership. As the candidates showed, what has been called "street smarts" is really a blend of charm, social savvy, determination, and persistence. Education also played an important part in many of the candidates' successes up to a point, but without the important "street smart" qualities just mentioned, it isn't sufficient to make a great leader.

There are a few key positive emotions and positive qualities such as optimism and persistence that account for a great deal more in business success than skill, education, and, to some degree, even talent; on the show we witnessed this in many ways as each episode aired. These positive qualities and personality traits make the difference between being tossed about by rough corporate waters or navigating a smooth course through turbulent times. Key traits like optimism, resilience, and emotional awareness are the navigational tools that steer the best leaders through even the fiercest storms. Cultivating these positive qualities does more than just alleviate work stress; when you're in a positive frame of mind you actually think in more productive and creative ways.[1]

Having resilience and an optimistic outlook creates subtle differences in the way exceptional leaders respond to both challenges and opportunities alike. This way of thinking builds strength by focusing on what is best in a situation and by downplaying obstacles. The practice and habit of adopting an optimistic outlook helps develop the core strengths of vision, resolve, and charisma—the three legs of the footstool that is the foundation on which excellent leadership is built.

> **Key traits like optimism, resilience, and emotional awareness are the navigational tools that steer the best leaders through even the fiercest storms.**

This book delves into those core components of leadership. The strength of vision refers to the creative, forward-looking, and hopeful ways an outstanding leader has of viewing the raw materials of any business opportunity. Resolve is the tenacity and self-control it takes to clear all the hurdles that are placed before any executive. And charisma refers to the intangible qualities that make a leader approachable, personable, and powerful.

The Apprentice candidates seem to be the lucky ones who are blessed with a strong natural level of optimism and resilience. They manage to turn the disappointments and setbacks of competition to their advantage, and they have gone on to do the same thing in their real-life careers. The stories about what happened to them before, during, and after the show reveal how they overcame adversity and used optimism as one of their most powerful tools. These positive qualities can be practiced and learned, and each chapter includes suggestions for building them.

When I first began my interviews with prospective candidates, I was suspicious that anyone could be so upbeat all of the time. As a clinical psychologist taught to help people overcome problems, it was slightly puzzling to me that they all had such a great outlook about life! As are most clinical psychologists, I was trained in the medical model of illness, and I wasn't as well prepared to deal with such buoyant personalities. During the selection process, I spent an hour with each applicant, getting a detailed life history. After a few accounts of "awesome" parents and idyllic childhoods, I was strangely comforted to hear that not all of them had picture-perfect experiences. As the days wore on, I heard stories of alcoholic parents, divorce, and even the loss of loved ones. This started to sound similar to the backgrounds I'd heard for so many years from clients.

> *The Apprentice* candidates seem to be the lucky ones who are blessed with a strong natural level of optimism and resilience.

There was one remarkable difference, however: the folks applying to the show had a great outlook on life, regardless of troubles they'd had along the way. They were too busy squeezing every ounce out of life to have come to see a therapist! I would never have met any of them had they not signed up to be a part of a new phenomenon, *The Apprentice*.

The world of psychology is just beginning to take note of positive qualities such as optimism, resilience, and life satisfaction. The picture that is beginning to unfold is that although these positive qualities are largely inherited, nevertheless, they are also skills that can be learned. We've known for quite some time that intelligence and proneness to depression have a strong genetic component, and the same seems to be true for happiness. If one identical twin is positive and bubbly, it is likely that the other twin will have the same disposition, but if the twins are fraternal (share only half their genes), they aren't any more likely to share a cheery disposition than by chance.[2]

Does this mean that if you were born with a gloomy disposition you are doomed to stay that way? Not at all. It may not always come naturally, but the habits of optimistic thinking can be practiced and learned, and with time, what starts as a habit leads to a genuine attitude change. There are many techniques, proven by research, that you can use to help yourself be more optimistic, even if you tend to be a little pessimistic by nature.

> It may not always come naturally, but the habits of optimistic thinking can be practiced and learned, and with time, what starts as a habit leads to a genuine attitude change.

What Are the Positive Emotions?

For many decades, the domain of therapists was largely to alleviate the suffering of those with mental illness. By focusing on these issues we've made great strides with improved medication and treatment for depression, anxiety, phobias, and attention disorders, to name just a few. Shelves of self-help books are full of sound and practical advice on easing the anguish of both the individual and the families of those struggling with problems in living. The price we have paid for this focus, however, is a scarcity of guidance about how to make life even richer. For many years that realm has been left to philosophy and religion.

In 1996, the president of the American Psychological Association at that time, Martin Seligman, called for research that would address mental health and the components of effective therapy. Since Dr. Seligman's presidency, the field of positive psychology, which addresses the positive emotions and qualities that propel us forward and add richness to our living, has blossomed into a legitimate and growing area of research with thousands of scientific studies lending credibility to its existence.

Positive emotions are those feelings that enhance our lives and give meaning and substance to both the good and the bad times we encounter in our day. This isn't the blind pursuit of hedonism or about how to numb and shelter ourselves from anything painful. Positive emotions give us an alternative to despair and, when practiced, lead to a well-earned strength of character. A short list of positive emotions includes happiness, joy, gratitude, courage, humanity, passion, and love. The positive emotions and qualities that relate to the business world include optimism, creativity, resilience, a balance between self-control and passion, emotional awareness, and sociability. Helping you to adopt these six positive qualities is the purpose of this book.

> Positive emotions are those feelings that enhance our lives and give meaning and substance to both the good and the bad times we encounter in our day.

Right about now you may be thinking that this all sounds a little too Pollyanna-like for the tough-minded world of competitive business. What about some pragmatic realism here? Of course, pessimism has its place and there are some jobs that absolutely require it.[3] For example, a trial attorney needs a healthy amount of worry and doubt about how hard it may be to convince a judge and a panel of jurors that her argument is a sound one. That motivates her to devote extra hours to preparation and research. But even the most cynical legal mind needs solid confidence and the positive belief that the case can ultimately be won.

The bulk of training in law school involves memorizing and practicing a certain type of logic, a new way of thinking. Reason and dispassionate logic are memorized, practiced, and driven home with an unsympathetic combination of lecture and theater. If you find yourself less than optimistic and confident in the world of business, you need to put yourself through a law school of sorts by learning a new way of thinking. Instead of ruthlessly attacking anything illogical and finding loopholes in the opponent's argument, you can learn to ruthlessly attack your own illogical thinking. In short, we can choose the way we think about things to ensure that we set ourselves up for as many opportunities as possible.

One of the most significant findings of psychology since the 1960s is that people can choose the way they think. Prior to that time, Freudian psychology dominated the field that was laden in determinism: the impressions laid down in early childhood firmly established a person's view of the world.[4] It wasn't until the advent of a new branch of psychology that studied cognition and learning that psychologists began to turn their attention from the unconscious, unrecognized material of the past to a person's current and conscious thoughts in the moment.

In the past forty years we've learned a great deal about how to modify the negative and nonproductive types of thinking that impact the way we feel, the choices we make in life, and the way we affect those around us. Sometimes these habitual unhelpful beliefs can be changed by learning new ways of thinking. In other instances, only emotions can change emotions, and it is the higher order, positive emotions that will bring about lasting change.[5]

The bulk of this book deals with the most relevant positive qualities for the business world and how this mind-set makes the difference between a merely successful career and one that is rich and deeply satisfying. Each chapter will draw on illustrations from *The Apprentice*, where a quality like optimism or resilience advanced a person and kept him from being fired. Although it is television, each episode contains a wealth of information about how different personality types fare in this competition that tests for interpersonal skills and leadership ability. The end of each chapter in this book contains proven techniques and skills that can be practiced to foster better leadership.

> One of the most significant findings of psychology since the 1960s is that people can choose the way they think.

Do Emotions Belong in the Workplace?

When we think about the word *emotion* in relation to the workplace, it conjures up unflattering images of losing control and breaking into a sweaty mess when the boss frowns and demands exact figures. Or it may bring to mind a time when a disapproving glance from a co-worker sent someone darting off to the nearest bathroom to fall apart in a moment of unflattering loss of control.

On *The Apprentice* there were times when tempers flared and things were said that didn't put people in their most favorable light, but this is not the same as recognizing and dealing with emotions at work. Displays of temper are frowned upon at work. Family might put up with it, but the people you work with aren't quite as forgiving when you hold your breath, stomp your feet, and sling insults at your office mate. None of these instances, however, has anything to do with using positive emotions in the work setting, and you can see why the word *emotion* gets a bad rap when it's associated with such erratic and unhelpful behavior. The kind of emotion that is good for business relates to an inner sense of well-being and a confident attitude that affects the way you view both the triumphs and setbacks that are part of everyday life.

> When we think about the word *emotion* in relation to the workplace, it conjures up unflattering images of losing control and breaking into a sweaty mess when the boss frowns and demands exact figures.

Of course, different types of work are more dependent on an optimistic attitude than others, and there are those jobs where it is ill-advised to be overly positive and confident. A financial adviser needs a healthy dose of trepidation and caution, especially when dealing with your grandmother's life savings! A safety inspector should be wearing the exact opposite of rose-colored glasses when determining if the building's elevators are safe. In leadership roles, however, just the opposite is true. Most positions that involve working with, leading, managing, or supervising people, and positions that require innovative and open-minded thinking are best served by resilience, flexibility, and amiability.

Many sectors of industry thrive on creativity and vision, and as we will see in Chapter 3, creativity is directly influenced by mood and emotion. Positive feelings stimulate the types of expansive and broadened thinking that lead to innovations like Post-it Notes and Super Glue. Researchers, developers, planners, and marketers all need this expansive and open-minded type of thinking to make such pioneering leaps and bounds.

When it comes to leadership, the difference between a "boss" and a truly inspiring leader is his or her ability to stay hopeful, to motivate others, and to be flexible and resilient in times of defeat. The stories of some of our greatest and most recognizable leaders feature many examples of how they used positive emotions. Eleanor Roosevelt is a classic case of optimistic leadership at its finest. She lived through an unpredictable and unhappy childhood with a cold and distant mother, who teased her for being "ugly," and an alcoholic father who was gone for long periods of time. Even as a child, Eleanor had an inner strength that allowed her to focus on the good times she had with her parents instead of the disappointments and heartbreaks. By the time Eleanor was ten years old, both of her parents had died. Despite all the losses she suffered, she excelled in school, eventually studying abroad in England. Several years after she returned from Europe she married her fifth cousin, Franklin D. Roosevelt.

> When it comes to leadership, the difference between a "boss" and a truly inspiring leader is his or her ability to stay hopeful, to motivate others, and to be flexible and resilient in times of defeat.

The same indefatigable spirit she had as a child served Eleanor Roosevelt later in her marriage, when she discovered her husband had been unfaithful. While the two of them drifted apart romantically, it only furthered her resolve to develop her own identity, and afterward she became more of a political and business partner to her husband. She devoted her life to her family, to human rights, and to social causes. She said, "You get more joy out of giving to others and should put a good deal of thought into the happiness you are able to give."[6]

Her compassion warmed the hearts of the country and her action inspired others to not give up hope. In 1936, four years after her husband was first elected as president, Eleanor Roosevelt gave a speech to a women's group and passed along some of the lessons she'd learned over the years: (1) Don't bear grudges; (2) Don't get discouraged too easily; and (3) Take defeat over and over again and pick up and go on.[7]

Through her husband's four-term presidency, Eleanor Roosevelt refused to be seen as a figurehead, insisting that she be treated instead as "plain, ordinary, Mrs. Roosevelt." When she died in 1962 at the age of seventy-eight, she left a legacy of her optimistic leadership style that had helped inspire a country though the Great Depression, the bombing of Pearl Harbor, and World War II.

> **Through her husband's four-term presidency, Eleanor Roosevelt refused to be seen as a figurehead, insisting that she be treated instead as "plain, ordinary, Mrs. Roosevelt."**

If you fast-forward to a more recent tragedy, September 11, 2001, you find another poignant example of positive qualities in leadership. Mayor Rudolph Giuliani showed that even the crustiest, hard-nosed, tough-talking politician (and former prosecutor) had the ability to give a grieving city and a grieving nation the hope that we could survive the attack on our country and on our sense of safety and security. On that terrible day while we watched our televisions in disbelief and horror, his words were a life raft in a sea of uncertainty. "Tomorrow New York is going to be here, and we're going to rebuild, and we're going to be stronger than we were before. . . . I want the people of New York to be an example to the rest of the country, and the rest of the world, that terrorism can't stop us."[8]

Giuliani told us what we feared the most, yet we needed to

hear the compassion and sorrow in his voice when he said that the number of casualties would be "more than any of us can bear." In the weeks that followed he attended as many funerals as the day would allow and let the families and the rest of the country know that we were all in this together. Speaking to the children in one particular service, he found just the right words: "Nobody can take your father from you. . . . He is part of you. He helped make you. . . . You have something lots of children don't have. You have the absolute, certain knowledge that your dad was a great man."[9]

Since the attacks, Rudolph Giuliani has reflected on the qualities it took to get him through those difficult hours, and he credits both strong convictions and a basic underlying sense of optimism. "Look, in a crisis you have to be optimistic. When I said the spirit of the city would be stronger, I didn't know that. I just hoped it."[10] He has also said that "You have to understand who and what you are" and draw strength from your core values to stay calm in a crisis. Giuliani's optimism, as you can imagine, isn't a Pollyanna point of view, but he has the ability to solve problems with a positive approach. "People follow solutions," he said. "If I said to you 'Things are very, very bad and they're going to get worse . . . follow me,' would you?"[11] He knows what many great leaders know: attitudes and emotions contain a self-fulfilling prophecy. That can-do spirit, especially in times of adversity and darkness, is the foundation that will rebuild our future and the legacy that has made our country great.

> "People follow solutions," Giuliani said. "If I said to you 'Things are very, very bad and they're going to get worse . . . follow me,' would you?"

The business world has its own legendary leaders who have acknowledged the power that emotional life plays in the world of commerce. One such legend is Jesse Livermore, who's considered to be one of the greatest stock traders of all time.[12] Known as the Great Bear, he understood the human element of Wall Street and made fortunes in the stock market even in the panic of 1907 and the crash of 1929. He made more than $3 million in one day in 1907, and he sold the market short and went into the Depression with $100 million in cash.

Although he had plenty to say about market timing and money management, the bulk of his advice to young speculators concerned human passion. He stressed that the stock market never changes because human nature never changes, and that it is emotion—not reason or logic—that drives the market. He was sensitive to the importance of emotional control and stated that it was the one essential factor in playing the market. He admonished would-be traders to use self-control and patience. In his early speculation days he had learned that the best strategy is to wait until the market gives you clues, signals, and hints, and not to feel rushed to act prematurely.

In stark contrast to his larger-than-life financial success, Livermore's personal life was tarnished by bouts of depression and scandal. There were opulent parties, yachts, mansions on Long Island and Palm Beach, and Park Avenue apartments, but he also had his share of troubles: three divorces, bankruptcy, and plenty of scandal. His weakness was beautiful women, and rumors of his liaisons echoed through the canyons of Wall Street. He also suffered from major depression, for which there was no treatment at the time. Although he took his own life in 1940, he'll always be remembered for the trading strategies that took him to the lofty heights he reached at the peak of his career. Positive emotions didn't play a role in his personal life, but he recognized that emotions have to be understood and harnessed before it is possible to speculate successfully. He was keenly aware of the effects of greed, fear, and hope when it comes to the psychology of the stock market, and that self-awareness led to his disciplined emotional approach that earned him his reputation as the world's greatest trader.

A more current role model of exemplary leadership is Louis Gerstner, the man who brought IBM back to the world of the living when it was headed for certain dissolution. The title of his account of the turnaround, *Who Says Elephants Can't Dance?* really says it all. Defeat was never an option for Gerstner, and his certainty that he could hold the company together and rebuild the leadership team was fueled by his positive attitude and his cool crisis management.

Before Gerstner arrived, most of the leadership on the inside of the company was resigned to carve the company into smaller units as IBM rapidly slid from its most profitable year ever in 1990 to a $16 billion loss by 1993. People who knew the company well were saddened by the impending demise of a true icon in the computing world, the company that led the computer revolution of the 1960s and 1970s with its invention of the mainframe. The media buzz was that IBM was finished as a force in the industry, and Bill Gates even predicted that the company would fold within seven years.

When Gerstner made the decision to leave his position as CEO at Nabisco and tackle the challenges at IBM, the prospect of saving the ailing company looked quite bleak. Early on he realized that instead of a new "vision," IBM needed to recommit to quality and to listen to their customers about delivering the performance they expected. He recognized that the human element of trust had to be reestablished if the failing company were ever to be saved. In just under a year he had managed to turn the fate of IBM around, and it was no longer sliding downhill. But now he had to ask himself if the company could ever become a leader again. The industry had moved away from IBM's strengths, and although the mainframe wasn't dead, the tide of business was rushing to individuals and small businesses, and that meant shifting from hardware to software. If they were to begin to compete in that market, the lineup of aggressive linebackers they would face would be daunting: Bill Gates, Larry Ellison, and Steve Jobs, to name a few.

Resilience is the attempt to overcome inevitable obstacles in life, and that is just what Gerstner determined to do one day while padding up and down a stretch of beach on the Florida Atlantic coast. He knew that there would be intimidating roadblocks ahead, but true to his positive nature he had the viewpoint that the challenge was what made it all the more intriguing. In that moment he determined not to be satisfied with simply bringing IBM back from the brink; he wanted to muscle it back to the top.

When Gerstner stepped down in 2002, the IBM workforce had increased by 100,000 and its stock increased in value by 800 percent. In the final analysis, he says that the most important element of transforming an institution is personal leadership and the passion of individuals. Although he says he never heard the word uttered at Harvard Business School, he has found that passion is the single most important element of personal leadership.[13]

> Gerstner says that the most important element of transforming an institution is personal leadership and the passion of individuals.

The concept of emotion in business is nothing new, and it encompasses the management of businesses both large and small, ranging from the political arena to the high-tech sector. An executive without a warm, comfortable, personable manner will ultimately struggle and find it difficult to inspire the confidence necessary to lead people effectively. Being at ease and approachable leads to better communication, lays the groundwork for trust, and helps executives make better decisions in difficult times. Just as it takes intelligence, practice, and study to learn the technical skills of developing strategies and time management, it takes emotional intelligence, practice, and willingness to develop the deeper and more subtle skills of compelling leadership. Although there may be such a thing as a "natural born leader," it is possible to learn and implement the skills of optimism, resilience, and other positive qualities.

The leader sets the tone for the group, even though the emotional climate is a subtle mix of everyone who is a part of the team. If a leader is distant, condescending, and unapproachable, the group will be frustrated and will likely spin its wheels instead of taking efficient action. An ineffective leader struggles with expressing empathy, yet the simple act of being heard, valued, and respected is what truly inspires people to do their very best at their job.

A leader who is uncomfortable with emotions or, worse still, who is hostile and authoritarian, will accomplish the exact opposite of the desired goal when it comes to motivating people. People who have to work for a hostile leader will respond in kind. Although they may not have the power and authority to respond directly to the hostile environment, they find subtle and passive ways of expressing their anger, usually through sabotage.

Leadership does involve "hard" concepts like vision, strategic decision making, time management, and tangible results, but emotions are often neglected and they are also basic aspects of leadership. The leader is the one who everyone looks to for safety, certainty, and inspiration—qualities that are less about technique and strategy and more about charisma and warmth. Psychologists and business leaders alike are beginning to research and document the "softer" aspects of leadership as they recognize the tremendous importance of a leader's personal qualities.

> **A leader who is uncomfortable with emotions or, worse still, who is hostile and authoritarian, will accomplish the exact opposite of the desired goal when it comes to motivating people.**

The Apprentice has proved to be a natural laboratory setting that depicts the dynamics of a work group and how individuals respond to various aspects of leadership. There are two competing groups with a different leader each week. This gives us a remarkable variety of leadership styles and group compositions to learn from. Because the candidates are living together and the stakes are so high, it is an atmosphere where emotions run wild, and the way the participants handle themselves and their relationships with each other is often predictive of their success.

> **Psychologists and business leaders alike are beginning to research and document the "softer" aspects of leadership.**

The Supernormal Profile

The television world of *The Apprentice* illustrates the power that personality and emotion wield when it comes to achieving success leading a group of people in the completion of a task. The people who populate this show are truly remarkable individuals with an impressive list of accomplishments. This strength of character is precisely what first sets them apart in the casting process and makes their tapes stand out among thousands that are stacked in the huge containers of mail. It takes a vibrant and over-the-top personality to wake up the poor soul in casting who has to view the homemade videos.

Underneath their vastly different outward appearances, many applicants share some common personality traits. A typical pattern of personality for someone who applies to *The Apprentice* is some mixture of enthusiasm, vitality, exuberance, sociability, and boisterousness. That's what makes the candidates so much fun to watch! A list of adjectives used to describe a typical group of candidates would read *bubbly, vivacious, delightful, high energy, talkative, always "up," driven, self-assured,* and *animated.* What is it that makes this group so upbeat? First, if you are a hardened pessimist, it isn't likely that you'll be sitting on your couch watching your favorite reality show and think, "You know, I would be great on that show. I think I'll apply right now!" Second, if you have the drive, ambition, and qualifications to aspire to be the next Donald Trump, it is likely that you haven't let setbacks get you down and you've had this positive attitude since you were fairly young.

> A typical pattern of personality for someone who applies to *The Apprentice* is some mixture of enthusiasm, vitality, exuberance, sociability, and boisterousness.

A personality profile typical of this group reveals a good amount of energy and enthusiasm and a notable absence of depression. For the most part, this group doesn't even register the usual range of blue days that most people sometimes experience. Dr. Richard Levak, a leading expert on personality assessment, brought me on board in 2001 to help him screen potential contestants for reality shows. Dr. Levak is one of those larger-than-life personalities, who creates a palpable buzz of energy when he enters the room. He works at a turbulent pace that is both exhilarating and slightly intimidating. He makes quite an impression, and more than one contestant has suspected him of being psychic, but he bases his observations on years of research and psychological data.

Richard has tested thousands of reality-show contestants and has written numerous books and papers on personality testing. In 2000, with the advent of a new genre of television—the reality show—Richard Levak was employed by various networks to determine whether an individual's personality type would be well suited for the unique demands of instant fame. Potential contestants had to be able to cope with the stressors of being fired or possibly rejected. In addition, once a show airs, they're subject to a lack of privacy, public scrutiny, hate mail, and websites that criticize their every move. The public tends to see contestants as characters rather than as real people who have careers, children, and family, so they feel free to make harsh judgments about them based just on their behavior on a television show.

Nevertheless, most candidates have remarkable ways of dealing with the negative press and seem to be able to take it all in stride. It quickly became apparent that this was an unusual group of people who have some distinctive coping mechanisms to shield them from the fickle world of Hollywood. It was initially difficult to convey this personality type to other professionals in the field of clinical psychology, however. Several years ago I attended a professional workshop with a group of psychiatrists, clinical psychologists, and therapists, and I attempted to describe to them this population that is blessed with such positive and resilient attitudes. Their reaction was one of skepticism and disbelief. Most of the professionals in the room wondered what these people were in denial about—what were they attempting to repress?

While the field of psychology lumbers into the twenty-first century dragging its heavy baggage packed full of determinism and mental illness, it is slowly making room for new models of behavior. In our line of work we seem to have accidentally stumbled upon a gold mine of human strengths and virtues. The profiles of the contestants are visibly different from the norm, and you can see the peaks and valleys that make them such an unusual group. After years of follow-up, it is evident that this isn't just a façade; this is the real thing and worthy of study. Dr. Richard Levak has coined the term *supernormal* to describe this extraordinarily durable and buoyant personality type. He notes that these reality shows can be a lot tougher than they seem, and that the contestants are "supernormal" when it comes to qualities like resilience and self-confidence.

> **Dr. Richard Levak has coined the term *supernormal* to describe this extraordinarily durable and buoyant personality type.**

Although most of the applicants who make it to the final rounds are gifted with exceptionally high levels of energy, enthusiasm, and happiness, they have varying degrees of skill and charm; those with the greatest repertoire of emotional skills quickly set themselves apart. The variability within the group makes it interesting to watch what happens when you put very talented, very smart, personable leaders together to be guided as a team by one of their own. Someone gets to take the reins every three days during an assigned competitive task. As each new season of *The Apprentice* airs, we gain a variety of examples of diverse leadership styles and varying amounts of optimism, resilience, sociability, emotional awareness, and emotional control. It is a great opportunity to examine the effects of various personality traits in positions of leadership.

Positive Qualities on *The Apprentice*

The candidates who make it on the show have a repertoire of emotional skills that have certainly helped them to collect their impressive list of accomplishments. From the first season of *The Apprentice*, Katrina Campins was in the top 3 percent of realtors nationwide, and that was at the ripe old age of twenty-four. Kwame Jackson has an MBA from Harvard and was working at the prestigious investment firm Goldman Sachs before entering the competition. Jessie Conners started a marketing management company for chiropractic offices at the age of seventeen, and at twenty-one, began investing in properties in Wisconsin.

From the second season of *The Apprentice*, Pamela Day has her undergraduate degree from Wharton School of Business and her MBA from Harvard. She invests in real estate and starts her own companies. Kelly Perdew was an Airborne Ranger in the U.S. Army and got his BS degree at West Point and his JD and MBA degrees simultaneously from UCLA. He has recently started a new business with Donald Trump involving a celebrity-branded direct marketing channel. He has also written a book about leadership and will soon be hosting a television show about the manufacture and use of innovative military technologies and hardware.

It's no coincidence that these superachievers share a personality profile of energy, warmth, passion, and optimism. They are people who don't take no for an answer and have a remarkable ability to infect others with their enthusiasm. Their performance illustrates the fact that these personal qualities do make a difference in how eager the group is to follow a given leader.

You too can improve your ability to motivate a group, inspire confidence, and overcome obstacles and setbacks. You can learn techniques to challenge distorted ways of thinking, identify limiting beliefs, and avoid personalizing. Sections of the book in Chapter 6 that pertain to group dynamics include tools for conflict resolution and better communication. Suggestions are also given for skills like breaking problems into manageable parts and discovering the ruts that could be draining your energy. Chapters 1 through 6 contain concrete examples and practical advice to improve the positive qualities that can enhance your leadership style.

CHAPTER TWO

Optimism: The Foundation of Success

The man who would succeed must think success, must think upward. He must think progressively, creatively, constructively, inventively, and, above all, optimistically.

—Orison Swett Marden (1850–1924), author and founder of *Success Magazine*; considered to be the founder of the success movement in America

FOR EACH SEASON *The Apprentice* has been on television, an ensemble of producers, doctors, psychologists, and casting directors has descended on a normally quiet hotel to conduct a final round of interviews to choose the characters who will appear on the show. The group of hopefuls submit to all sorts of poking and prodding, as every nook and cranny of their lives is examined in an attempt to select the right individuals.

The applicants, most of them energetic extroverts, are happy to recount their childhood, family, and high school experiences. The pattern that has emerged in these interviews—and what is most strikingly uniform about their outlook—is the positive light they cast on their varied life experiences, both good and bad. Looking back, they remember their disappointments and setbacks with the conclusion that things always worked out for the best. For the most part, I have found that this cheerful outlook holds up under the rigors of filming and public scrutiny that constitute this reality-show experience.

Bowie Hogg, the fourth person to be fired on the first season of *The Apprentice*, had perfected this type of sunny outlook. He burst into a room, so eager to chat you'd think he hadn't seen people in weeks. Bowie is a big guy, about 6 feet 2 inches. He hails from Dallas, Texas; is totally at ease with strangers; and is one of those folks who chat with the cashier, the waitress, the bus driver— just about anyone he meets. Part of his charm stems from his southern Texas upbringing and some from the larger-than-life characters in his family background.

> Looking back, they remember their disappointments and setbacks with the conclusion that things always worked out for the best.

Bowie Hogg's great-grandfather's cousin was Texas's first native-born governor in the late 1800s. Governor James Stephen Hogg was also 6 feet 2 inches and weighed 285 pounds. There is a statue of the governor in Austin, and Bowie says he hates to admit it but he "does resemble him!" Governor Hogg had a daughter named Ima Hogg (Bowie swears this is true), who is recognized as one of the greatest philanthropists in the state of Texas. Bowie's parents are named Porky and Sue Hogg (again, believe it or not!), and Bowie glows when he talks about their work as teachers, their positive attitude toward setbacks, and the loving atmosphere they created for their children.

It would be natural to wonder if Bowie ever got teased in school for his name or his size. He said he'd always received a

Bowie Hogg, the fourth person to be fired on the first season of *The Apprentice*, has perfected an optimistic outlook.

lot of attention, but he explained that it just showed how much everybody liked him. One of his classmates from Texas A&M remembered that Bowie was the kind of guy everyone wanted to get to know and that no one ever had a bad thing to say about him. Now, you would suspect that such a positive attitude would be the result of a charmed life, but Bowie's family has had their share of tragedy. His grandparents and uncle were both killed by a drunk driver when his mother was quite young, and in 2000, his second oldest brother was killed by another drunk driver. During the gathering at their house after the funeral, a family friend remarked that the family seemed so happy. Bowie said that they were grieving in their own way, but that it was important to all of them that they stay upbeat. Bowie's family believes that you can make it through anything if surrounded by the people who love you. Even now, he isn't bitter or angry about what happened to his brother, and he says that the tragedy brought him closer to the people he loves and the experience gave him an appreciation for his many blessings.

Bowie's cheerful outlook came through the night he was fired. His response was, "Nobody died, did they? Hey, Donald Trump just told me I was a great salesman. What could be wrong with that?" Instead of interpreting being fired as a defeat, he saw it as a terrific bit of luck that he had even been chosen to be a part of the show, and he was certain that his involvement would help him with anything he chose to do in life.

Although Bowie didn't get a chance to be a project manager, his teammates looked to him for motivation when things got tough. Donald Trump said that the firing wasn't an easy decision. He told Bowie that he had many strengths and was impressed with his performance. Trump later told George Ross (Trump's attorney and "right-hand-man" in the boardroom) and Carolyn Kepcher (the other member of Trump's boardroom advisory panel and chief operating officer of Trump National Golf Course) that he really liked Bowie, but he didn't think that he had presented himself as well as his teammates had. And Bowie realized he had been up against two very poised and polished speakers, both of whom ultimately made it to the final four.

> **Optimism is contagious; it creates an upward spiral of positive expectations and infects others with the possibility of success.**

Optimism is contagious; it creates an upward spiral of positive expectations and infects others with the possibility of success. Bowie's optimistic outlook colors his interpretation of loss and disappointment. He doesn't carry grudges; in fact, he is reliably cheerful and pleasant. People are drawn to him and he helps create an upbeat and motivated team in the work setting. His optimism also influences his expectation of success, and he assumes that things will continue to go well.

Of course, optimism isn't always the right tool for every job; sometimes a skeptical outlook is called for. Dr. David Gould, from season one of *The Apprentice,* has earned a reputation as a reliable and successful venture capitalist through his realistic assessments of the probability of entrepreneurial success. David earned an M.D. from Jefferson Medical College and an MBA from New

York University. His astute and pragmatic view of the task his group was given, and his standing on the team, was realistic, and perhaps true, but not particularly optimistic.

Both teams for that episode of *The Apprentice* were assigned to get "back to basics" and sell lemonade on the streets of New York City. One team was composed of all men and one team of all women. The men's team chose the South Street Seaport Village, in downtown New York City, as a good tourist spot to set up their lemonade stand. But while it sounded great on paper, the location smelled of fish and wasn't particularly attractive or appetizing for lemonade sales to visitors. David quickly realized that with their chosen location, their odds wouldn't be good. David said that it was "late in the day and I was already certain the women would win." No matter how true that observation might have been, a team needs to keep the faith. David's team did lose to the women, which meant that someone from the men's team would be fired.

Each week, the losing team's leader must select two team-mates, and all three of them must attend the boardroom, where one of them will be fired. David was selected as one of three candidates to go to the boardroom. Trump hadn't yet hit upon the short and simple directive "You're fired," so he explained to the three candidates that there were two elevators, one that went back up to the suite and one that went down to the street, and with that he sent David home.

> Leadership and team motivation, however, often don't rely on realism; team members need optimism, even when signs indicate they should abandon their efforts.

David's gritty realism is exactly what makes him so valuable as a venture capitalist. His job requires that he make tough-minded assessments of the products and services of startup companies in the healthcare services. There are huge amounts of money on the line in this field, and that money may be tied up for a long time, so investors count on people like him to be sober and realistic about prospects for lucrative returns on their investment. David's is one of those jobs that requires critical thinking and a keen eye on what can go wrong. Other fields that call for sober realism are accounting, the law, insurance, tax auditing, and quality control.[1] Leadership and team motivation, however, often don't rely on realism; team members need optimism, even when signs indicate they should abandon their efforts. The very outlook that serves David so well in his job doesn't apply well to team motivation.

Is Optimism Founded in Reality?

Optimism tends to lift the mood of other people while pessimism seems to depress it, so it's easy to see its effect on a group or team. And beyond the gestalt of a group, there are individual tasks that benefit from a positive outlook—for instance, jobs in sales and marketing or research and design. Although pessimism doesn't necessarily lead to depression, pessimists have been found to be up to eight times more likely to become depressed in adverse situations; have poorer physical health and shorter lives than optimists; and tend to have rockier personal relationships.[2] But is pessimism more grounded in reality than optimism? In a clever study designed to measure the effects of mood on perception, undergraduate students were classified as depressed or not depressed (because of the correlation between pessimism and depression it was assumed that the depressed group gave more "pessimistic" explanations) and then were given varying degrees of control in a task involving turning on a green light with a button. In one condition, the light came on predictably each time the students pressed the button. In another condition, it didn't matter if the students pressed the button or not—the light would randomly go off and on. When the students were asked to estimate how much control they had over the light, the depressed students were accurate for both conditions: having control and not having control. The not-depressed students were right about the amount of control they had when they actually did have control, but when they really had no control they still judged that they had control about 35 percent of the time.

An authority in the field of positive psychology, Martin Seligman, sums it up best when he says that the depressed group in this study was "sadder but wiser." Happy, more optimistic people fall back on their past positive experiences so they think that things will usually work out and that they have control in reaching their goals. Their experience has always been one of efficacy, so they rate their control in a positive light. They were accurate when they had control, but even when they had no control they judged a high amount of control. Pessimists are more skeptical and fall back on past negative experiences when things didn't work out. Consequently, pessimists were more accurate when it came to both conditions: control or no control.[3]

If being pessimistic is more realistic, does this mean that being optimistic is being just plain "dumb and happy"? If someone is overly cheerful, is it because he isn't bright enough to know how bad it really is out there? Evidence that you can be both smart and still quite happy comes from a study that found that, in a group of elderly people who lived in a residential assisted living home, a greater number of residents with higher childhood IQs had a more optimistic point of view.[4] Researchers measured the level of optimism and absence of depression and anxiety among these senior citizens, and the results showed that those with the highest childhood IQs also rated their quality of life the highest, or most optimistically.

> Happy, more optimistic people fall back on their past positive experiences so they think that things will usually work out and that they have control in reaching their goals.

But a positive viewpoint is a lot more about attitude than it is about intelligence. People make a conscious choice to be hopeful. Part of being successful in life is being flexible enough to choose a point of view that best matches the task at hand. If you are auditing a company's books, anticipating a difficult exam, planning your long-term investments, or betting your life's savings at the blackjack tables, a more pessimistic outlook will best guide you and keep you out of trouble.[5] If, however, you are tasked with motivating and leading others, it will matter that you look at any setbacks as temporary and that you maintain hope and confidence, even when the outlook seems bleak. We look to a leader for guidance, reassurance, and the subtle cues to determine if we should be confident or worried, if we should give up or persevere.

> **Part of being successful in life is being flexible enough to choose a point of view that best matches the task at hand.**

Let's take a look at the effects of optimism on both the group and the individual level, and see the remarkable impact created by a positive frame of mind. At the end of this chapter you will find suggestions for becoming a more optimistic leader.

The Turkeys and the Eagles Are Among Us

Besides being the story of a dysfunctional family, with a father giving his two sons mixed messages about the rights and wrongs of life, Arthur Miller's play *Death of a Salesman* is the tale of a man who loses all hope.[6] Willy Loman, the main character, is a traveling salesman who boasts to his sons about his big dreams, but in reality he is insecure about his prospects, uncertain if people like him, and he gets easily discouraged and jealous of others' success. For these reasons, he has never been a very good salesman.

The play opens on the last few days of Loman's life, when he has been fired from his job and is utterly broken and defeated. As he begins to lose touch with reality, he has imaginary conversations with his brother Ben, whom he idolizes. The two brothers' lives are in sharp contrast: Willy lived a small and disillusioned life while Ben went to Africa and became rich mining diamonds. In one of the dream scenes, Ben appears to Willy and says, "The jungle is dark, but full of diamonds, Willy." His words don't have the intended impact; Willy continues to see the darkness in his own life, not the bright and lustrous possibilities that exist. It seems too late for Willy, as his last few chances at greatness slip through his fingers.

Being in sales takes a pretty thick skin and a good dose of determination.[7] You have to keep getting back up after you've been knocked down by rejection and overcome by pressure. Does a person's degree of optimism have an impact on his success? For instance, why is it that the top 20 percent of a typical sales force captures about 80 percent of the sales?

> Being in sales takes a pretty thick skin and a good dose of determination. You have to keep getting back up after you've been knocked down by rejection and overcome by pressure.

Picture two cubicles side-by-side, two different salespeople poised for the day's business: headsets in their ears, a cup of Starbucks on each of their desks, and their computer screens giving off a bluish glow. Both have the same pension plan, the same years of experience, and have dozed through the same motivational seminars the company offers every year. The only difference between the two salespeople is that one is thinking about all the times she made the sale while the other is dwelling on all the people who hung up or said no. Will their bottom lines be any different at the end of the quarter? That is exactly what Metropolitan Life Insurance Company wanted to know in the early 1980s.

At that time, the insurance business was booming, yet Metropolitan Life Insurance was losing large amounts of money in hiring costs every year. The head of the company, John Creedon, was perplexed at the turnover rate of agents in the sales force. Potential employees went through a long process of tests and interviews and then were put through extensive training, yet 50 percent quit in the first year and at the end of four years a full 80 percent were gone. It cost more than $30,000 to hire and train each agent, so the net loss per year was close to $75 million. The emotional toll was high as well, leaving the agents who didn't succeed and their supervisors with a bitter taste of failure.

John Creedon wanted a way to weed out the people who wouldn't fit, and he suspected it had something to do with the amount of rejection that's involved in sales. You get ten rejections for every yes; it takes a lot of persistence to keep stepping up to the plate after so many strikes and fouls. Creedon had seen Dr. Seligman speak about the differences between an unwavering pessimist and a resolute optimist, and he was curious about whether those qualities could be identified and corrected. He suspected that a pessimist would tend to get discouraged after all of the rejections, and he wanted to know if there was a way to recognize the pessimists before they were hired as sales agents. In doing so, they could steer susceptible individuals away from a career that would be emotionally costly to them and wasteful for the company.

Dr. Seligman and his associates began by giving the test of optimism (the Seligman Attributional Style Questionnaire, or SASQ) to two hundred experienced sales agents who had already been identified as being either "turkeys" or "eagles," the former being pretty unproductive and the latter being top performers. As expected, the eagles had much higher scores on optimism than did the turkeys. As a matter of fact, those with the higher scores outsold the more pessimistic sales agents by 37 percent in their first two years of work. Even more impressive was the difference between the most extreme types: those in the top 10 percent for optimism outsold the most pessimistic bottom 10 percent by 88 percent!

It looked like they were really on to something, so they began testing for optimism in the hiring process as well. Out of 1,000 newly hired sales agents who passed the Career Profile (a test published by the Life Insurance Management Research Association and a standard for the industry), half were identified as optimists and half as pessimists. This large group of new hires was called the "regular force," but the company also created a "special force" of 129 agents who had just barely failed the industry standard but had very high scores on optimism. Over the next two years, the company followed the agents' progress, and at the end of the second year the most optimistic among the regular force sold 31 percent more than the pessimistic group. The performance of the special force followed the same trend, even though these agents wouldn't have been hired at all exclusively using the industry standard. At the end of their second year, the special force outsold the pessimists in the regular force by 57 percent!

The company executives were convinced that this measure was valuable for determining their sales force and they responded by changing the hiring practices. They began using the SASQ to screen all new applicants and those in the most pessimistic 25th percentile weren't hired. Additionally, those who barely failed the Career Profile (Met Life required a score of twelve) but had a high score of optimism were hired. By adopting this new hiring policy, Met Life increased its sales force to more than 12,000 and increased its share of the personal insurance market by nearly 50 percent.[8]

> Most of the contestants have said that they would compete in the show even if there were no money involved.

People like the "eagles" believe that every no they hear moves them a step closer to yes. *The Apprentice* cast is full of that type of optimist, who sees "no" as a challenge rather than as a rejection. They truly love the idea of transactions, and indeed, many of the episodes have showcased their talent in salesmanship. After all, they are trying to impress Donald Trump, who relishes "the art of the deal." They've hawked lemonade; a brand of bottled water called Trump Ice; new flavors of ice cream, toothpaste, and cleaning products; as well as artwork, restaurants, apartments, and advertising. The show often focuses on the competition between contestants, so viewers don't always get to see how exhilarated and animated these people are at the prospect of making a deal.

Most of the contestants have said that they would compete in the show even if there were no money involved. Their mentor, Donald Trump, echoes the sentiment, noting that "money was never a big motivation . . . except as a way to keep score. The real excitement is playing the game."[9]

An Optimistic Attitude Sells Itself

The most exciting sales pitch for the people on *The Apprentice* is what they say to promote themselves in the boardroom. Salesmanship and optimism are intricately linked in business and in life because we are, in a sense, always selling ourselves. It takes self-assuredness and talent to maneuver boardroom politics when the whole point is to find fault with the team that failed in meeting the challenge. Andy Litinsky and Raj Bhakta, from season two, were both experts at selling themselves in the boardroom, and they did so with their unwavering positive beliefs.

Raj was only 28 years old when he was on the show, but if you closed your eyes and listened to him talk, you would swear he was much older. Early in the season, he wore a red velvet suit with oxford shoes and carried a walking stick! His air of superiority is actually quite charming, probably because it is born out of self-confidence rather than insecurity or disdain for other people.

Raj does not suffer from a moment of self-doubt. His attitude is part born and part bred, and he is a delightful by-product of his father's Indian culture and his mother's Irish heritage. He was the treasured eldest son, with younger sisters to dote on him, and as if that wasn't enough, he had a surrogate grandmother nearby who used to tell him he would grow up to do great things. Raj's confidence didn't falter when his team, Mosaic, lost the ad campaign for a spot to recruit for the NYPD. The other team had chosen to slant their campaign toward a personal heartfelt approach, while Raj steered his team toward a military theme. Donny Deutsch, a well-known figure in the advertising world, had the ultimate say and he chose the other team's concept. During the boardroom, most of Raj's team members admitted that they thought their ad was too militant and wouldn't be as effective a recruiting tool as a more emotional spot. On *The Apprentice*, it's very rarely clear-cut who should be blamed for a bad idea when the whole team has worked on the project, but in this case it was clearly Raj, who had come up with and pushed for the military slant.

So, it wasn't looking good for Raj. However, he stood his ground and said that, frankly, he thought the other team's spot was "too soft" and he maintained that he still liked his own idea better. He sold himself and sold his idea, even when it had failed; and although he was a clear choice to take the fall, he was spared that night. Trump praised him for standing his ground and sent someone else home instead. Indeed, someone with less self-confidence and optimism could easily have been defensive or unclear about his decision, but Raj stood by his beliefs and was respected and admired for it.

> An optimist expects positive outcomes and usually gets exactly what she is anticipating; when she doesn't, it isn't taken personally.

That solid belief in yourself and lack of self-doubt is magnetic, in both business and one's personal life. An optimist expects positive outcomes and usually gets exactly what she is anticipating; when she doesn't, it isn't taken personally. Because the focus isn't on failure, success is more likely the next time because an optimist will just keep trying.

Andy Litinsky was another cast member from season two who in the boardroom seemed to be made of Teflon: none of the accusations his teammates made seemed to stick. At the time the show aired, Andy was 22 years old and just about to graduate from college. A national debate champion from Harvard, Andy was eager to get into the boardroom and showcase his skills. Each time his team lost, he was singled out as being too young, too inexperienced, and too uncertain about taking action. But Andy came alive in the boardroom; you could tell he was having fun with the verbal sparring. Some seasoned business veterans fell before he did, and his unflagging certainty that he could talk his way out of a rough spot was just about all he had during some of the meetings.

There is an element of luck involved in navigating *The Apprentice*, but both Raj and Andy stayed in the game a little longer because of their conviction that they deserved to be there. This optimistic ability to sell ideas and yourself is an important tool in success. Indeed, optimism is the foundation of self-confidence. Leaders must be able to infuse a group of people with hopeful expectations and excitement about a project. *The Apprentice* candidates are an especially difficult group to manage—the smart and talented Type A people who make up the teams don't respond well to poor leadership. And the situation actually isn't that different

> **This optimistic ability to sell ideas and yourself is an important tool in success. Indeed, optimism is the foundation of self-confidence.**

Andy Litinsky, from season two, was a national debate champion from Harvard.

from many of today's corporate settings, which are composed of well-educated, demanding, and talented employees.

Leading the Type A Personality Calls for Optimism About People

Technology has caused an evolution in the workplace whereby the focus of business now is on innovation and change.[10] With a highly educated and technically skilled workforce, a company has employees who often know more about their jobs than does the CEO and they want their thoughts and ideas to be heard. The tide has turned; we've moved from an industrial economy to a knowledge economy, and today's successful leaders must attract and retain talented people to compete in this environment. Leadership in this world of mavericks and constant change requires confidence, charisma, and people skills. In fact, the reasons for a senior executive's failures rarely involve technical incompetence. Even the most conservative academics at Harvard University have determined that much of a leader's performance can be explained by personal qualities like charisma and people skills.

> **Leadership in this world of mavericks and constant change requires confidence, charisma, and people skills.**

Confidence, charm, and sociability are qualities that *The Apprentice* candidates have in abundance. Indeed, they need those qualities to fall back on as they face challenging tasks and competitive cohorts. When they step up for their chance at leadership, they face the same dynamics a CEO faces in an organization that thrives on intellect and skill. The teams on *The Apprentice* are composed of very bright and talented individuals who want to be recognized for their talent and who can't be led by threat or intimidation. An effective leader needs to recognize the abilities of team members and keep them motivated and encouraged.

On the first season of *The Apprentice*, Nick Warnock took

the lead on a particular task after nearly being fired for work on a previous task. Trump said he wanted to see Nick in action because he was curious to observe his leadership skills. Early in the morning the two teams listened as their next assignment was explained: their mission was to feature an artist's work in a gallery exhibit, and the team with the most paintings sold would win a reward and an exemption from the boardroom.

With his poise and public-speaking skills, Nick is the consummate salesman, but the world of fine art was unfamiliar territory for him. Even so, he kept his cool smile when the assignment was announced. Each team visited four artists to preview their work and ultimately choose one artist to feature. Whereas the other team made what seemed to be a logical decision based on high price potential, Nick went with his gut: he was convinced that the artist he liked was the best choice for the assignment. Half of his team adamantly opposed his choice and were quick to point out that art appreciation was not Nick's forte. But with a firm, almost parental look at his team, he stuck with his decision. Although his team had strong opinions, they needed Nick to stay confident and self-assured while respecting their input, and that is exactly what Nick did.

Nick directed the team to work quickly to set up a wine and cheese table and print flyers for the gallery opening. Nick moved through the gallery with ease, never getting flustered and surveying every detail, from the platters of fruit and cheese to the soft lighting on the artwork against the weathered brick background. Every time a team member would catch his eye, Nick would break into a warm smile, looking every inch the winner even before a patron entered the gallery. Nick selected two more experienced team members to explain the artwork to the visitors, while he introduced patrons to the artist. Nick was reassuring when a team member had doubts that night and said in an even and relaxed voice, "We're gonna be all right." True to his words, the team achieved an overwhelming victory by selling more paintings and earning more money.

Optimism can truly outweigh lack of experience, and with

Nick's positive attitude, the absence of an art background couldn't get in the way. Regardless of his lack of expertise, team members looked to their leader to set the tone, to give the task meaning and direction, and to gain trust and a sense of hope. Nick won the task with an assuring smile and the belief that they could win. He recognized that the task was just as much about working together confidently as a team as it was about selling art.

Good leadership is something that goes on among people; it isn't something that is done to them. Each member of a group influences the others in subtle ways as together they reach a consensus on the right course of action. Yet none is more influential in setting the mood, tone, and productivity of a team than the person in charge. Chris Russo, from the second season of *The Apprentice*, grew up not far from Nick Warnock on Long Island, and he has that same unwavering conviction that puts people at ease. Both gentlemen also come with a sales background in which a positive frame of mind is especially important.

> **Good leadership is something that goes on among people; it isn't something that is done to them.**

Chris is by nature an optimist whose life story demonstrates his tenacity and good spirit. His mom was a single parent who provided plenty of love but had to work hard to make ends meet. Chris can't remember a time when money wasn't exciting to him. In fact, he had a saying in grade school: "Life is money; money is life." He hid his money under the rug, but then decided to stash his thirteen single dollars in the dictionary because he wanted them to be crisp and flat.

During the casting process, Chris stood out right away. He's a warm and colorful self-made entrepreneur, and the combination of an Italian heritage and a New York accent only enhanced his appeal. Once his teammates got to know him, they were convinced that he deserved a walk-on role on the TV series *The Sopranos*. During an *Apprentice* task to open a restaurant starting from scratch in only two days, Chris's optimistic outlook helped keep the team laughing and motivated.

From Chris's work managing new stockbrokers at the firm where he works, he recognized the importance of attitude; when the project manager placed him in charge of customer service for the restaurant, that assignment was a natural for him. Because all the team members had been living together in such close quarters, he knew they had a lot of preconceived notions about him, especially because of his accent and "colorful language." To get beyond those prejudices, he recited his repertoire of curse words, got everyone laughing, and when he was finished, they were open and receptive to the advice he gave about working with customers in the food service industry. With his team of Type A leaders, he could just as easily have offended them by coming on as "the expert," but instead he used humor to put everyone at ease so that they wouldn't be defensive.

Chris pulled each person aside to let him know what good qualities the individual had and how those could help the joint effort. He helped buoy everyone with his optimism and light-heartedness. At one point during the opening night, one of the patron's paper menus caught fire from the candle at the table, but the team handled the emergency with good humor, a reflection of Chris's influence. In fact, the opposing team had worked with one of New York City's top chefs, but that asset was no match for the lighthearted enthusiasm of Team Mosaic. The team's playfulness warmed the atmosphere and helped create the right ambience. It was the patrons' ratings for the *Zagat* dining guide that determined the winner that night, and that right ambience helped Chris's team to win.

> The most effective leaders expect success and always anticipate a positive outcome.

In sharp contrast to the winning attitude Chris showed on the restaurant task, he's the first to admit that he was later fired on a different task because, as the leader, he didn't rally hope and enthusiasm for the project. Chris was tasked to run a bridal store for a day—and for that job, he was a fish out of water.

The most effective leaders expect success and always anticipate a positive outcome. Most times that is the way Chris looks at things, but on that particular task he was expecting defeat. Not only did he feel ill-suited to run a bridal shop, but the leader of the opposing team ran a bridal store for a living. Thus Chris's team noticed that he was losing steam, and so it was hard for them to stay energized and committed. When Chris looked back on the task, he knew he hadn't given his normal level of passion and action. The glass just wasn't half full to him that day, and his outlook cascaded into defeat and his firing that evening. In the boardroom that night, after Chris had been fired, Donald turned to Carolyn and George and said that it had been a tough decision and that he had no doubt that Chris would be "very successful."

It is that attitude of optimism that can make the difference between igniting the passion of the team members and not having enough energy to stay the course. Today's work environment makes good leadership more challenging than ever. People are more educated, more intelligent, and more prone to challenge authority than they were several decades ago. Information that used to be accessible to a few select individuals in a company is now available to everyone on the Internet, and along with being better informed, employees want more voice in the decision-making process. Workers no longer tolerate being dictated to but instead require their leaders to persuade and inspire them in a way that makes them want to follow. The subtle nuances of leading highly skilled people persuasively require a great deal of confidence, a certainty that helps the team keep the faith, and the ability to see a clear course of action.

Self-Confident Leadership Is Most Effective

From the Trump Towers to the local midwestern Home Depot, truly successful organizations are built around leaders who are guided by an attitude of confidence and certainty. Some of the theories of good leadership and effective management place leaders and their followers in quadrants, with the idea of matching the right leadership style to the needs of the individual. Although a perceptive leader should be responsive to the unique needs of those they lead, an optimistic approach goes a long way toward satisfying the most basic expectations, no matter what quadrant the employees are in.

Group dynamics, whether in a corporation, association, club, or sports team, create a need for someone to infuse the members with a sense of purpose and the confidence and trust that if everyone works toward the goal, together they can achieve their purpose. Finally, the members of the group need hope and confidence to carry them through both the small successes and the failures that the group will encounter along the way. Purpose and direction that is optimistically conveyed by the person in charge can light a fire of conviction in everyone involved. It's what Disney's Michael Eisner calls a "strong point of view."[11]

When you work on a project, it's difficult to clearly see the endpoint and determine the right steps to take to get where you want to go. When you look back, the correct direction seems crystal clear, but the water is often murky in the beginning. In the Air Force's twelve-week Officer Training School, held at Maxwell Air Force Base in Montgomery, Alabama, an Officer Trainee (OT) who doesn't have a clear picture of the mission is called "OT Clueless." It's unlikely that a candidate with that title will ever be allowed to graduate from the leadership training.

Through this murky water the exemplary leader navigates the crew with a sense of unshakable faith and certainty. This leader has the psychological tenacity that allows her to be confident in herself and in those around her. That confidence acts as fuel to ignite the energy and untapped resources of the team. When the group members sense the confidence their leader has in them, the result is a self-fulfilling prophecy that, in turn, influences the outcome of the project. To the hardened realist, such optimism may seem unwarranted

> When the group members sense the confidence their leader has in them, the result is a self-fulfilling prophecy that, in turn, influences the outcome of the project.

and unrealistic, but if it generates enthusiasm and brings about results, does that really matter?

The glue that holds a team together is pretty much the same, regardless of personalities and work settings. Psychologist Abraham Maslow was a pioneer in the application of psychology to the work setting, and he is most famous for his "hierarchy of needs," which defined the drives and needs that motivate an individual.[12] In this hierarchy, safety is the primary need, which sits at the base of Maslow's pyramid; the optimistic leader taps into this need and meets it with clear directions and confidence.

Developing an Optimistic Attitude

In any hotel conference room across the country, on any given day of the week, there will probably be a business seminar being conducted against a backdrop of brocade wallpaper and before banquet tables lined with pastries and coffee. The traditional courses in these seminars are on dealing with difficult people, conflict resolution, and innovation, along with courses covering harder-to-define work qualities like passion, hope, and emotional intelligence. Although a personal quality like optimism may seem a difficult thing to learn, adopting this attitude can be achieved with practice.

Having an optimistic attitude is largely a matter of how you choose to explain the events of your life. If you believe that a failure or a mistake is personal (you blame yourself for a setback), permanent (you believe the hardship is here to stay), and universal (you believe that if one thing goes bad,

> Although a personal quality like optimism may seem a difficult thing to learn, adopting this attitude can be achieved with practice.

others will follow), it impacts your mood and your outlook in an adverse way. Optimists believe that missteps are temporary; they tend not to blame themselves for the misfortune, and they know that although they may get knocked down in one area, that setback doesn't pertain to other aspects of their lives. In other words, they hold the belief that setbacks are limited, specific, and related to some external cause. They don't internalize or blame themselves when things go badly.

Pessimists, on the other hand, can be extraordinarily tough on themselves. When they have a failure, they convince themselves that things will never get better. This type of thinking can lead to depression, to feeling trapped and powerless to change the course of events in your life. As a leader, you can spread that feeling of hopelessness quickly to and through a group, stopping the project's momentum in its tracks. Optimism is the gas pedal and pessimism is the brake. You can develop a more optimistic leadership style by revising the way you explain both the good and the bad events in your life.

> You can develop a more optimistic leadership style by revising the way you explain both the good and the bad events in your life.

Discover Your Attitude Style

Thankfully, just because you are predisposed to a certain way of looking at things doesn't mean you are doomed and determined to follow that line of thinking forever. You can do a great deal to shift your attitude in the direction that is most likely to lead to success. And when it comes to leading people, the attitude of choice is one that people will want to follow, and no one wants to follow the voice of doom.

At the end of this chapter there are specific steps you can follow to practice being more optimistic. But if you're not sure how you view life, take an online test at foresightonline.com to measure your own level of optimism. It will take about 15 minutes and the cost is about $20, but it will give you insight into your attitude style, along with specific suggestions for changing areas that are as yet undeveloped. But if you intend to take this test of optimism, do so before you read the next section, as you may be able to "read into" the questions once you understand the following explanation of attitude styles, which will skew the results.

Our Explanations of Life's Events

Most of us have a pretty consistent style of reacting to the ebb and flow of life, both the big stresses and the bothersome daily hassles we encounter as a result of rolling out of bed. The way that we react to and think about these events affects us mentally, emotionally, and even physically. Researchers studying fibromyalgia (a particularly painful form of muscle and joint pain along with fatigue) have found that the daily irritations of life, combined with the way that people interpret those annoyances, directly relates to the level of physical pain they experience.[13] Tension and the ups and downs of life affect our moods and our physical well-being. Although it is nearly impossible to avoid hassles in life, you can shield yourself from being overly affected by them: the explanation you give to the experience makes all the difference.

> Although it is nearly impossible to avoid hassles in life, you can shield yourself from being overly affected by them: the explanation you give to the experience makes all the difference.

When we explain something unfavorable that happens to us, we determine (1) whether we take it personally, (2) how permanent we think it is, and (3) whether we think it will affect other areas of our lives. The most pessimistic person tends to look at failure and say, "I really screwed up, it's permanent and I'll never recover from it, and this will probably happen with other things I try." The most optimistic person will look at failure and say, "It isn't anything about me

> The most optimistic person will look at failure and say, "It isn't anything about me personally, it's only a temporary setback, and this is just one little area of my life."

personally; it's only a temporary setback, and this is just one little area of my life."

The Optimistic Explanation

An explanation for bad events involves three dimensions: personal, permanence, and pervasiveness.[14] Our perception about the cause of such events falls somewhere along a continuum as follows:

Personal   Internalized _____ Externalized

Permanence   Permanent _____ Temporary

Pervasiveness   Global _____ Specific

If you are the hopeful kind of person who explains a setback as something external ("bad timing" or "they were in a bad mood"); temporary ("tomorrow is a new day"); and specific ("this is just this one instance"), you'll find those explanations shield you from getting depressed about the misfortunes of life. An optimist's explanation of misfortune falls on the right-hand side of the continuum. It is also the attitude that uplifts and inspires other people. For example, the politicians we're most likely to elect pepper their speeches with humor, hope, and a focus on the positive.

So, when it comes to holding on to those hopeful feelings, the reasoning we use about the good events that come our way also affects how we feel. In this case, the dimensions of an optimistic outlook are the same, but reversed:

Personal   Externalized _____ Internalized

Permanence   Temporary _____ Permanent

Pervasiveness   Specific _____ Global

Think about the last time you got a raise or promotion. Did you look at it as well deserved (internal) or just dumb luck (external)? Did you believe that you'd continue to move up (permanent) or that this would be a one-time event (temporary)? Finally, did you think that you'd achieved something that would favorably change other areas of your life (global)? Whether you are talking about misfortune or blessings, optimists tend to choose the most favorable explanation for the situation. They tell themselves that they got the contract because they were prepared and had a stellar presentation; if they didn't get the contract, they reason that the client had a temporary lapse of judgment and made a bad choice.

It may sound unrealistic, even dangerously self-deceptive, to pursue optimistic thinking, and of course this assumes that you are responsible enough to know when you need more training, better presentation skills, or more experience. But, when it comes to motivating yourself or others, consider what Winston Churchill said when he declared, "I am an optimist. It does not seem too much use being anything else."

Putting the Cart Before the Horse

When you choose to adopt the more positive point of view, it doesn't guarantee wealth, fame, beauty, or success, but it does increase the likelihood that you'll be persistent. Many of the legendary successes in business have been realized at the end of a long string of defeats. For example, Colonel Sanders is said to have offered his recipe for fried chicken to thousands of vendors before someone finally took the chance on his idea.

> Being an optimist or a pessimist is a preference, much like being predominantly right- or left-handed. You can learn to use the other hand, but it requires patience and hard work.

What if you took the test online and found that your score wasn't as high as you'd like, or if you intuitively know that you lean toward a dimmer shade of disposition? Being an optimist or a pessimist is a preference, much like being predominantly right- or left-handed. You can learn to use the other hand, but it requires patience and hard work. In the beginning it may feel a little awkward, but once you realize that it is a choice, you simply "fake it till you make it." This is a situation where you want to put the cart before the horse; in other words, positive feelings of hope and optimism aren't preceded by certainty—sometimes you have to step out on faith.

For example, Nick Warnock had that type of positive faith during the art gallery task. When he gave a reassuring smile to his team before the event started, he really had no clue if the gallery show would be a success, and he had no real reason to be certain that his team would win. He simply took a leap of faith and his team took the leap with him.

It's a simple concept, but it can be difficult to put into practice. The pragmatic realist inside says, "Show me the proof first, then I'll believe it can be done." Another small, superstitious voice says, "If you prepare for the worst, at least you won't get disappointed by failure." That can be a great strategy if you are preparing for a tax audit or taking the bar exam, but think of the risk you assume when it comes to staying motivated for the long haul. An extreme but illustrative example is the way various people respond to a diagnosis of cancer. If they are realistic about the sobering statistics, they might decide it wise not to hope for recovery. If instead, they choose to favor the growing body of anecdotal reports concerning the effect of attitude on illness, they might choose to affect the outcome of the illness. Even doctors often are puzzled about the possible outcome: it could go either way, but what does it hurt to choose faith?

On an optimism scale from 1 to 10, with 10 being the highest, a friend of mine named Football Sparks would have rated a 10 +. He was the janitor for a law firm in Cincinnati, Ohio. The partners of the firm paid him handsomely to change light bulbs, do a little dusting, and take out the trash occasionally, but everyone knew that his real job was to lift people's spirits. He had nicknames like "Diamond Lil" for every person in the firm. You could hear him coming down the hall, with a whistle, song, or a chuckle. Even though life had not been easy for him, he was always in a good mood.

During WWII, Football Sparks had been part of an African-American battalion that went on ahead to pave roads for the rest of the troops. It was quite a dangerous job, as they ventured into areas that were heavily occupied. Many of his good friends died, and though he sensed that they were sacrificial lambs, he never held that against anybody. When he came home, instead of a hero's welcome, he found that there were still certain water fountains he couldn't drink from, and he wasn't allowed in many restaurants in the city. Still, he never seemed to resent these slights and he used his charm and bubbly good nature to make a pretty good living as a shoeshine man on the streets of Cincinnati.

One of the partners of the law firm took a liking to Football, and asked if he'd like a job at the firm. But years later, people quickly noticed when he wasn't quite himself and saw him stop to lean on a windowsill as he made his rounds. Always a hefty guy, he began to look a little drawn and lost some weight. Everyone was saddened to hear that he had cancer of the lymph nodes.

In the hospital, Football was a favorite of the nursing staff, and he still managed to spread good cheer from the confines of his bed. When I left the firm, Football had finished his treatment and was recuperating at home. I kept tabs on him over the years and was pleased to hear that he was healthy and happy, back to making his rounds and flirting with the paralegals. Ten years later he finally retired, but during his bout with cancer he had more than enough optimism to go around. Football was never one to let on when he was feeling tired or worried; he "faked it" from one day to the next, until he was back on his feet and spreading good cheer again.

> When you choose to explain events in an optimistic light, there is an element of risk that you'll be proven wrong, and just like anything of value, it requires courage to take a risk.

When you choose to explain events in an optimistic light,

there is an element of risk that you'll be proven wrong, and just like anything of value, it requires courage to take a risk. Of course, there are times when sobering realism overshadows the stance that this is the best of all possible worlds. Like Pangloss in Voltaire's *Candide*, it is irresponsible and ridiculous to ignore poverty, corruption, disease, and all else that is wrong with the world. But having a positive view that even these problems can be eliminated just might help make that happen.

Somehow, *The Apprentice* candidates have a natural gift for looking at life in just this way. It probably explains why they have the motivation to apply for a competitive show like this in the first place, and moreover, it gives them an innate sense of leadership ability and a risk-taking spirit that allow them to gamble big and win. Not only does this stance toward life pay off big in the corporate world, but it also affects your personal life.

Optimism Outside the Boardroom

Optimism is central to how we feel about life, how satisfied we are with our friends and family, our jobs and hobbies, and our future. People who are optimistic are content with their relationships because their focus is on what is good in other people. They tend to not hold on to grudges. Furthermore, satisfied, optimistic couples have a "romantic illusion" about each other. They see virtues in their partners that other people don't see, and they focus on the strengths of their relationship rather than the weaknesses. Optimism may not sound very objective or realistic, but it works to keep couples happy and together. (Of course, if your partner is demeaning, or worse, abusive, that is not the quality you want to romanticize.)

Most of the candidates who apply to be on a reality show have enviable marriages. They certainly don't mirror the 50 percent divorce rate that exists in the general population. Although we can't say that their optimistic attitudes caused their low divorce rate, we can speculate that the way they think about and subsequently relate to their partners has had a positive effect.

An added benefit of having an optimistic attitude is improved health. We've long known that depression inhibits a person's immune system and contributes to illness, especially chronic, stress-related disease, but research has now established a solid link between positive attitudes and good or improved physical health. There are all sorts of health benefits to having a sunny disposition, and a person with this outlook is more likely to heal from a whole host of medical problems—everything from radiation treatment during cancer to rehabilitation after orthopedic surgery.

> **There are all sorts of health benefits to having a sunny disposition, and a person with this outlook is more likely to heal from a whole host of medical problems.**

Doctors are beginning to realize that a patient's belief system is an important factor in recovery, especially how effectual the patient believes he can be in his recuperation.[15] When it comes to otherwise healthy individuals, the optimist is at an advantage with a full host of long-term health benefits, such as a slower heart rate and increased lung capacity, even among those who smoke![16] Although I definitely wouldn't recommend picking up any new vices to get you through the years, assuming a hopeful outlook can contribute to a long and happy life.

In a study of the habits and attitudes of people who lived to be over 100 years old, researchers had a hard time attributing that longevity to any of the usual suspected factors. These people didn't necessarily drink, smoke, or eat any less than the people they outlasted, but they did have a remarkable philosophy about life. Most had survived friends, spouses, and even children, but they maintained a wise and upbeat attitude through it all. At the end of this chapter, you'll find the Subjective Happiness Scale devised by Sonja Lyubomirsky, an associate professor at the University of California at Riverside. Take the questionnaire to determine your own level of happiness. Then, if you'd like to be a bit more encouraging, upbeat, and inspirational, follow the steps in the next section to practice and learn the skills of optimistic thinking.

The Guide for Optimistic Leadership

Initial Steps

Spend some time each day reviewing any setbacks you have encountered. Write down the negative thoughts that come to mind. Hint: They usually take the form of thoughts like this:

I have failed.

These things *always* happen to me.

This is so unfair. Why can't *life* be easier for me?

Notice that the first example deals with personalizing, the second with permanence, and the third with pervasiveness. Now, have a good argument with yourself. Rewrite each thought from an optimistic viewpoint. By doing so, you are challenging the automatic, gloomy thoughts that habitually come to mind. Eventually, you will be able to practice thinking this way without having to write it down, but for now invest the time in a good pen and notebook.

Then go over the list in these ways:

- Edit the list, watching out for personalizations, "fortune-telling," or "all or nothing" statements.

   Examples: "I am never going to get over this sales slump" is an example of "fortune telling" and relates to permanence. "I didn't make this sale so my career is over" is an example of "all or nothing" thinking and relates to pervasiveness. Rewrite the statement to reflect a more positive approach wherever you find one of these "cognitive distortions."

Examples: "This was a tough organization to make the sale to, but there is a better market I can find." "The audience wasn't in the proper mood for that particular presentation."

- Argue with yourself over the particularly troubling beliefs on the list by writing down answers to the following. For illustration, I show a possible response to an item that says, "After the mistake I made, the boss doesn't have confidence in me anymore" (a combination of a personalization and "fortune-telling):

    What is the evidence? ("He ignored me when I made a suggestion about finding new accounts.")

    Are there any alternative explanations? ("He has been really preoccupied lately with a new proposal.")

    If this is true, what is the worst that could happen? ("He might replace me.")

    What is the effect of the thought? (For example, "It makes me angry," or sad, or happy, or will probably lead to not working as efficiently.)

    What could I do about it? ("Send him a written proposal so he has time to think about it." Or "Talk to him about what happened.")

    What would I tell a friend who faced this same problem? ("I would tell her that she has always done a great job and it is more likely that the boss is just not himself.")

- Take action steps. Rewrite an explanation—a nonpersonal, specific, and temporary explanation for what happened.

    Example: "The boss has been preoccupied (nonpersonal), and it this is the first time he hasn't really considered one of my suggestions (specific), and when he isn't so preoccupied I can present it again (temporary)."

Remember that this is a new skill and getting used to it will take some practice, so be patient and don't expect to change your automatic thoughts overnight. If you take the time to write things down, however, you can speed up the process.

Further Steps

- **Have a sense of humor.** Having a fun-loving, humorous appreciation of life is incompatible with a gloomy, pessimistic outlook. If you find that this is a neglected part of yourself, identify what you need to create more balance. Do you need to take more time for yourself and your family? Are you still enjoying your job? Can you still see the humor in everyday situations? A good sense of humor puts people at ease, minimizes stress, and diffuses conflicts. One of the less well-known secrets of successful business leaders is that they get people to laugh![17]

- **Are you having fun yet?** You may not need much prompting to think about ways that you could add more fun to your life, or you may be so entrenched in productivity that you'll have to actually schedule your fun time, but either way, it is a remedy for a pessimistic outlook. Just in case you are hopelessly out of touch with your playful side, here are some ideas:

  Visit the zoo.

  Eat an ice cream cone.

  Rent a funny movie (the old Pink Panther movies work quite well).

  Try out a climbing wall.

  Go roller skating.

  Play a board game.

- **Set aside some time to go on a fun retreat.** There are many types of retreats designed to shake things up and get you out of the rut that is draining your energy and keeping you from having a more positive outlook on life. Some ideas are:

Outward Bound, www.outwardbound.com; 866.467.7651. Outward Bound is a wilderness adventure that combines physical and mental challenges to stimulate you to overcome rigid and unproductive attitudes and beliefs.

Art and Soul, www.artandsoulretreat.com; 503.695.5332. Art and Soul is a retreat with dozens of workshops, including quilting, carving, painting, weaving, and sewing, designed to energize your creative spirit and reveal the secrets of your soul.

Wild Women Expeditions, www.wildwomenexp.com; 705.866.1260. Wild Women Expeditions, which offers canoe trips, sea kayaking adventures, and other activities in northern Ontario, is designed for fun, adventure, relaxation, and appreciation of the natural environment.

Going Beyond

Changing the style you use in explaining the events of your life is just one way to develop a more motivating and optimistic outlook. After you've identified some of the less productive ways you've been thinking about things, you can move on to improve your overall outlook. A primary skill that many of the reality-show contestants possess is the ability to focus on what is right instead of all that may be wrong. Fine-tuning a sense of gratitude goes a long way in shifting your focus from the setbacks of life to all of its blessings. It is a seemingly small modification, but one that enriches not only your own life but the lives of those you touch in your home and workplace.

One particularly upbeat and bubbly *Apprentice* contestant confessed that she was really quite unhappy with her job. When I asked her how she managed to maintain the bright façade, she said that at the end of every day she drew up a list of things she was grateful for, such as getting to talk to her grandparents or enjoying the scenery on her drive to work. She titled the list "Ten Things That Were Good About Today." Try it yourself. Although it takes a little practice, slowly shift your attitude from disappointment to gratitude. The first time I tried making a list such as just mentioned, I got stuck on number 7 and left the list on my desk. My husband, Tony, is a naturally optimistic person, and the next time I looked at the list he had filled in the three blanks for me.

Developing the habit of showing gratitude will also make it easier to motivate those around you, especially when the going gets tough. Acknowledging the help you've received from others will pay big dividends, both at home and at work. The following Subjective Happiness Scale devised by Sonja Lyubomirsky[18] will give you an estimate of your own subjective level of happiness.

Subjective Happiness Scale

For each of the following statements and/or questions, fill in the circle for the point on the scale that you feel best describes you.

1. In general, I consider myself:

①   ②   ③   ④   ⑤   ⑥   ⑦

Not a very happy person   A very happy person

2. Compared to most of my peers, I consider myself:

①   ②   ③   ④   ⑤   ⑥   ⑦

Less happy   More happy

3. Some people are generally very happy. They enjoy life regardless of what is going on, getting the most of everything. To what extent does this characterization describe you?

①   ②   ③   ④   ⑤   ⑥   ⑦

Not at all   A great deal

4. Some people are generally not very happy. Although they are not depressed, they never seem as happy as they might be. To what extent does this characterization describe you?

①   ②   ③   ④   ⑤   ⑥   ⑦

A great deal   Not at all

To score the test, total your answers for the questions and divide by 4.

If you find that your score is 6 or above, you are probably one of those naturally optimistic people who tends to look on the bright side.

If you scored anywhere between 3 and 6, you may be fairly happy most of the time, but may have some situations where you would prefer to be happier.

If you scored below 3, you may struggle with pessimism and may find that you have periods of being "blue" where you tend to personalize setbacks and think that when bad things happen, they will not change for the better.

The mean for adult Americans is 4.8. Two-thirds of people score between 3.8 and 5.8.

Although most emotional states can be changed, a trait or tendency like optimism or pessimism is largely genetic. That does not determine how unchangeable that tendency is, however, and although some traits like intelligence are more difficult to change, traits like pessimism are very changeable. If you practice the suggestions given in the previous exercise and retake the test, you may find that you can improve your score.

CHAPTER THREE

Creativity: Adding Value to Your Work

Every human being has the instinctive need for the highest
values of beauty, truth, and justice. . . . If we can accept this
notion, then the key question isn't "what fosters creativity?"
but it is why in God's name isn't everyone creative?

—ABRAHAM MASLOW, *Maslow on Management*

ASIDE FROM TIME CONSTRAINTS and limited resources, the
tasks on *The Apprentice* are made even more challenging because they all require "out of the box" thinking. Creativity has
distinguished Mark Burnett, the show's creator and producer,
from the crowd, so it is no wonder that it figures so prominently
in his show. For example, candidates are required to develop advertising campaigns, create new products, and even design new
video games, and creative thinking is important to advance to the

position of the final Apprentice. During season three, an unflappable mother of two made it all the way to the final two, despite the fact that she didn't have a college education; it was her unique style of problem solving that led to her successful track record.

Season three pitted "book smarts" against "street smarts." Tana Goertz was the last person remaining from the "street smarts" team in the final boardroom. Although she wasn't chosen as the final Apprentice, Donald Trump praised her for her great track record and her creative thinking. Among other things, although her teammate created the actual product, Tana developed the idea for a CD-like pamphlet as part of the advertising assignment for Pontiac, and the company loved it so much they decided to use it in their actual sales campaign. She also helped design a turnstile for office clutter and a tee-shirt with "bedazzled" rhinestones, and named a new pizza "Mangia Meatball." Not one to rest on her laurels, Tana created a children's book during the time the show was airing so that she would be able to share it on her press rounds after the finale.

Season one also had its share of creative candidates. Jessie

Although Tana Goertz wasn't chosen as the final Apprentice, Donald Trump praised her for her great track record and creative thinking.

Conners, in particular, had a knack for innovation and creativity. She grew up in a rural area of northern Wisconsin, where her parents elected to have her home-schooled. The source of her learning was the farm on which she lived and the world of her imagination. Her brown eyes have a sparkle of excitement that promises fun and mischief, and her mouth is always turned up in a knowing smile.

Jessie was the sixth person to be fired during season one, and although she didn't advance as far as she would have liked, she was extremely successful at a very young age. Only twenty-one years old at the time of the show, she had already created a lucrative marketing service for chiropractors in her hometown. Jessie realized that most doctors focused on their medical training, so they don't have much business acumen. They would enter private practice and struggle to pay their school loans, not because they weren't good

> Donald Trump places great emphasis on novelty and creativity in his business dealings; indeed, deals are his "art form."

at what they did, but because they lacked marketing and business expertise. Jessie offered them some clever ideas for attracting patients, and was soon in demand with many of the local practitioners.

But Jessie had devised unique ways to make money even as a child on her farm. She started her own country store and sold eggs at a roadside stand just outside the family's property. She once found a dead porcupine in the woods in back of the house. When her uncle told her that porcupine quills were in demand, she tugged and tugged to release them but couldn't loosen them, so she ran back to their barn for a pair of pliers. She soon had hundreds of beautiful black and white porcupine quills, and the next day she set them out for sale at her roadside stand. Jessie was insulted when someone wanted to pay her twenty-five cents for each quill—she had set the price at a dollar each—so she has the quills to this day. Jessie has turned her creativity into success in both real estate and marketing.

Donald Trump places great emphasis on novelty and creativity in his business dealings; indeed, deals are his "art form." His ability to see new opportunities where others don't keeps him a few steps ahead of the pack. For example, long ago he bought property along the Hudson River on New York City's Upper West Side that was not desirable to other investors. At the time it was a dingy waterfront and marina area, and the elevated Henry Hudson Parkway obstructed the water view for any new buildings that could be built there.

Trump had the idea to build a high-rise apartment complex that would offer prime unobstructed views of the river. He had snatched up quite a bit of property, and he slowly began building a long line of apartment buildings bearing the Trump Place emblem. They quickly began to fill up, even though the view of the river is framed by the parkway. In the interim, the waterfront was renovated, and now there's a beautiful park with baseball fields, dog parks, running trails, and quaintly lit tree-lined paths. He added a Trump Market for upscale shopping, an in-house dry cleaning service, and fitness centers to serve the residents. This is now prime real estate in New York City.

> Not everyone has the inherent ability to come up with technological innovations, or to invent new products, but there is a basic level of creativity that anyone can achieve through practice.

In short, ten years ago, where others saw a run-down waterfront and a noisy parkway, Trump imagined the possibilities. He was right, and his gamble paid off. When he sees this creative quality in others, he instantly recognizes and admires it. Most of those selected to compete for *The Apprentice* have that innovative ability.

So you see that creativity is more important than ever in our economy. Indeed, ideas are among a company's most valuable commodities. Not everyone has the inherent ability to come up with technological innovations, or to invent new products, but there is a basic level of creativity that anyone can achieve through practice. Although you may not be the next great poet or artist, your creativity is vital to learning and to remaining open to new ideas, no matter what your line of work.

Creativity also contributes to good leadership. Executives who become too linear in their thinking and get stuck in a rut can fall short of meeting the demands of the job, not because they lacked the skills but because they failed to recognize a novel idea. Creativity is also closely related to optimism; the group dynamics of creativity ignite the fire that spreads positive feelings and innovation.

The Roots of Stifled Creativity

Where does creativity come from? What is it about some people that encourages them to churn out ideas almost nonstop while others only rehash old ideas? Yes, some people are smarter or quicker than others, and they have novel ideas and see opportunities where others do not. But we all have the capability to be creative to some extent; in fact, later in this chapter ("The Guide for Creative Leadership" section) I talk more about how you can choose to be more creative—changes you can make in your life that will help you release the fresh ideas and novel thoughts that are inside you. But before we start that, let's first look at conditions that squelch creativity, both in individuals and in team efforts.

Negativity and Self-Doubt

We are all born with the ability to be creative. But our experiences in growing up and our outlook on life can make us pull back into our shells, crushing the natural creativity in us. Indeed, creativity can easily be stifled by self-doubt and negative thoughts. Although self-doubt has many sources, the people we love and trust can cause us to second-guess or doubt ourselves.

In the early 1960s, a powerful social experiment was conducted that was a little off-color ethically, but it provided insight into social dynamics. In a film documenting the study, a second-grade class sits quietly as their beloved teacher tells them about a discovery that children with blue eyes are smarter than children with green or brown eyes. She is going to give them colored armbands so that everyone can tell the difference. Minutes later on the playground, without any prompting, the children divide their play into groups. Old friendships are severed, and the "green and brown eyes" children begin to participate less while the "blue eyes" children thrive. Also, in the classroom, the children in the "green and brown eyes" group who had previously made straight As start doing poorly on their tests, while those in the "blue eyes" group begin getting better grades despite previous poor performance.

> Creativity can easily be stifled by self-doubt and negative thoughts.

The next morning, the teacher tells the class that there had been a mistake: the children with green and brown eyes are really smarter. Then the roles are reversed, with the "blue eyes" children becoming dejected and earning poorer grades than the day before. By lunchtime, the researchers realized that the study worked all too well and they brought it to an abrupt end. The children were told the truth, and a long debriefing took place about how it felt to be in an outcast group. Researchers today would not be permitted to repeat the experiment, but it taught those earlier researchers, not to mention the children, not only that we can easily be taught to be prejudiced but also that we are quite susceptible to what we are told about our abilities and our worth.[1] If a teacher tells his children how stupid and inferior they are, he is likely to get the performance to prove it.

Simple negative comments can be the beginning of a dangerous downward spiral and a lifelong tendency for a negative outlook. On the other hand, positive comments can inoculate us against negative outside forces. Self-confidence leads people to try new ways of doing things and thinking creatively. For example, the contestants on *The Apprentice* are self-confident and self-assured, which fuels their creative, entrepreneurial spirit.

Pamela Day, from the second season, is tall, confident, sophisticated, and accomplished. She stays cool and unruffled, and she seems able to rise above the noise to stay focused and open to new opportunities.

> **Self-confidence leads people to try new ways of doing things and thinking creatively.**

Pam likes to create business ventures. Her raw material is investments, and she pieces together opportunities that others may not see. Her business Crimson Holdings was created from scratch and is named after the colors of her alma mater, Harvard Business School. Beginning in 1999, she assembled a group of engineers to build a vision for a software product she had. The product would track how employees used their computers and other software. The company became Blazent and was backed by top-tier investment groups. Immediately afterward, she assembled a group of investors for a venture into real estate in the booming San Francisco economy, and ever since has discovered prospects that others might not see. Even after she had been fired from *The Apprentice*, she quickly came up with five or six new ideas she'd had for business ventures while participating on the show.

Pam's success is directly a result of her knack for novelty. Even her speech is peppered with novel words and witty sayings, and she is always fast on her feet.

Her creative ability is a combination of her natural skills and her background. Growing up in the rural equestrian neighborhood of Colt's Neck, New Jersey, Pam had a pretty simple childhood during which she was always challenged to do her best, yet always appreciated for her talents. She notes that her parents always encouraged her and her brother and sister to excel. At the dinner table, the family talked about science, math, and history. She was given new challenges such as learning to ride a horse, playing an instrument, or studying a new language. Pam had an inner sense that everything would work out for her, and she learned to speak her mind, trust her own ideas, and not be easily

Pamela Day, from the second season, is confident, sophisticed, and accomplished.

swayed by the opinions of others. Her positive frame of mind led her to be broad-minded and creatively expansive in her thinking. She trusted her instincts and tried new things. These habits stayed with her through undergraduate school at Penn and Harvard Business School. She laughs easily, takes calculated risks, and truly enjoys her work and her life.

Lack of Spontaneity

If a company doesn't want its workers thinking outside the box, daydreaming, or being distracted when adding up columns of numbers, simply create the most somber mood possible. Nothing kills creativity like the standard gray furnishings from an office supply store. In some office settings, the only brightly colored object is a splash of day-glo Post-it Notes or paperclips stashed in a magnetic holder.

But it isn't just the setting of business institutions that saps our creativity. The suppression of creativity can begin in grade school, when we are admonished to "stay in the lines" or use our right hand. Schools like the Montessori, in contrast, are carefully structured to foster learning without sacrificing creativity. They offer children as many options as possible. For instance, Montessori schools recognize that children have different levels of energy, so they designate a large square on the floor as an "action" area. Students who feel like they need to let some energy loose can go into the square and jump rope or do jumping jacks rather than wait for the recess period. The underlying message is that the children learn to trust their own senses, to think for themselves, and to have individual ideas.

> The suppression of creativity can begin in grade school, when we are admonished to "stay in the lines" or use our right hand.

In stark contrast to the free spirit of a Montessori school, many academic institutions can be dangerous places for a creative spirit. Some of the most successful business leaders instinctively seem to have shied away from too much education, recognizing that they work best in flexible situations and with spontaneity. It isn't the learning process itself that stifles expanded thinking, but the surroundings and the way a class is taught.

When it comes to tasks that call for creative thinking, for example, writing, making big life decisions, or coming up with a new marketing idea, you can be more imaginative in surroundings that will boost your mood. Arrange your setting so that you have lots of fresh air and sunlight if possible. People who live in rainy climates can use lighting that will mimic sunlight and is available online. Create a comfortable atmosphere with bright colors, flowers, or music. Surround yourself with other positive, uplifting people.

Industrial psychologists have studied the effect that color, lighting, and general office environment have on productivity, and they have found that different kinds of work call for different environments. For example, the industrial psychologists of the early 1900s studied assembly lines and factory work, and pointed out that diversions were likely to cause accidents and reduce productivity. They thought it better to have a drab environment, with no windows, and the right type of lighting that would keep people alert and focused on the task at hand. But an unpleasant side effect of this atmosphere is the negative mood it creates and its influence on people's ability to think in new and creative ways. A positive atmosphere, on the other hand, fosters an expansive mental set and primes people's ability to be open to new experiences and ideas.

> A positive atmosphere fosters an expansive mental set and primes people's ability to be open to new experiences and ideas.

With changes in technology, the old concept of the industrial assembly-line type work has been altered. The manufacture of goods is largely computerized and automated. Rather than merely supervise work being done or enforce rules, managers today, especially those in roles involving leadership, need to be innovative thinkers and be able to adjust methods and make rapid changes in order to compete. Many of the major think tanks, such as those at IBM and Apple, recognize the impact that environment has on creativity, and they have designed their buildings to be colorful and stimulating. Indeed, the bridge between a cheerful setting and a creative output is an optimistic, happy mood. An employer can paint the office bright yellow, but it's the positive outlook he expresses that makes the difference.

Pessimism

We've discussed optimism in Chapter 2, but it bears viewing here in relation to creativity. In a cleverly designed study, researchers have made a solid case for the role of positive emotions in stimulating creative thinking. Researchers gave subjects in the study a box of matches, a candle, and some thumbtacks, and instructed them to find ways to attach the candles to the wall so that the candles wouldn't drip (the study was conducted before dripless candles). The group that was first put into a good mood by watching cartoons and eating candy was more likely to think of creative ways to attach the candle to the wall without it dripping, such as emptying the box of matches, tacking the empty box to the wall, and using the melted wax to secure the candle inside the box.[2]

"Happy" teams have been found to work faster and better on creative tasks than control groups who weren't first put into a happy mood.[3] The theory is that a positive mood leads to expansive and broadminded thinking while increasing the members' tolerance and patience for each other. In another study, "happy" groups were found to be much better and quicker at creative tasks such as using materials to create a lunar hotel out of index cards, masking tape, a ruler, scissors, and crayons. The researchers compared the appearance of their subjects' creations but also their durability as a way of judging their overall effectiveness. The groups that had been put into a good mood made more attractive and more functional products. The researchers noted that the groups in positive-mood condition were more likely than the control groups to work cohesively and gained more from brainstorming, as well as more tolerant of others' ideas.

> Many of the major think tanks, such as those at IBM and Apple, recognize the impact that environment has on creativity, and they have designed their buildings to be colorful and stimulating.

This simple study helps explain why an optimistic leader is able to better foster group cohesion and creative momentum. A gloomy tone decreases the likelihood that members with share their ideas. A positive tone creates an atmosphere of acceptance and allows the crucial process of brainstorming to take place.

The Sparks That Ignite Creativity

A memorable character of the first season of *The Apprentice* is Troy McClain, the cowboy from Boise, Idaho, who charmed his way through twelve episodes. Sayings like "happier than a pup with two peters" roll off his tongue, and he seems never at a loss for words. Some of the more hardened New Yorkers didn't buy his routine, but he eventually won over even the most cynical with his dimpled, ruffled appeal. Troy's story illustrates that a sense of humor and good mood can spark creativity.

At home, Troy has always been a hero to his mom and his baby sister. The fact that he had to become the man of the house very early on doesn't strike him as a setback or a burden. When his dad left, he simply stepped into the role and happily watched after his sister, who is hearing impaired and developmentally challenged. He counts that fact as one of his biggest blessings in life. He felt responsible for providing for his family, so Troy abandoned his dreams of college and started working right out of high school. During *The Apprentice*, Troy competed against Harvard MBAs and an M.D., but with his wit and creativity he outlasted eleven other competitors.

One of Troy's most innovative moments even piqued the interest of lawyers around the nation. Troy's team selected him as project manager for a task to renovate and rent an apartment in

Troy McClain, from season one, outlasted eleven other competitors.

New York City. Both teams had forty-eight hours and seed money to complete their project. It looked rather grim for Troy's team as Katrina Campins, the leader of the opposing team, had been named one of the top thirty realtors in Miami and Troy had only dabbled in real estate up to that point.

Troy and Katrina previewed both properties: both were in desirable locations, but one was in slightly better condition. Katrina knew right away which apartment she wanted but asked Troy coyly which one he wanted. When he replied that he wasn't sure, she suggested they settle it by writing their choices on pieces of paper. Katrina wrote down the address of the location she wanted, but Troy simply wrote, "I want what you want." Since they both wanted the same property, the result was left to the toss of a coin. As luck would have it, Troy won the toss. His team used lots of paint and elbow grease, and managed to get it rented for more than the other place, thus winning that round. After that show aired, Troy received e-mails on his website from attorneys around the country who were quite impressed with his strategy.

Even in the most serious of situations, Troy keeps his sense of humor; there seems to be a joke about to bubble up in him at any moment. In fact, his levity is a lightning rod for great ideas and his sense of humor keeps his surroundings positive and enhances his creativity. In another episode, the task was to sell Trump Ice, a new line of bottled water. Even though the pressure was on, Troy was still in good humor and as he rode in a cab to a restaurant, he stared out the window, and in one of those Eureka! moments, he shouted out that they didn't have to just sell pallets of the bottled water they had on hand. They could sell a year's worth at once, to be delivered at scheduled times throughout the year. Even though he wasn't project manager for that task, his team won that one, too. Troy's good spirits helped give his team a creative edge.

A sense of humor helped the men's team on season two, when their spirits were up and the opposing team was sinking under the weight of discord. A happy team is a team that knows its munchies. It was men against women, with the exception of one man on the women's team and one woman on the men's team. The fighting on the women's team was particularly bitter, while the men's team seemed to generally be having a good time.

Their second task was to create a new flavor of ice cream, have it made, and then see which team could sell the most. The women came up with an interesting and exotic flavor, "Red Velvet," but the men hit it out of the ballpark. When someone on the men's team suggested what became their winning flavor during a brainstorming session, the big question was, "Why hasn't this been marketed before?" In this case, it was to stick with classic vanilla, but add the "lightning bolt" of crumbled Dunkin Donuts. The flavor sold as fast as the team could dish it out, and Dreyers Ice Cream Company was quite pleased with their new flavor. For this project, the relationships among members of the two groups created two very different moods. Infighting on the women's team stifled their creativity. But brainstorming in a lighthearted atmosphere freed up the men's team to toss out crazy ideas and led to more possibilities than they would have come up with individually.

> A sense of humor helped the men's team on season two, when their spirits were up and the opposing team was sinking under the weight of discord.

The creative spark can come from a group of lighthearted guys but it can also come from several members of a team who are having fun. Late in the season of the first *Apprentice*, teams were tasked to sell rickshaw rides in Manhattan. The directions were pretty open-ended, and each group was each given a team of rickshaws, operators, and seed money. In that crucial brainstorming process when the tone of the group is so important, one group had an extra dose of lightheartedness, thanks to a little chemistry between two members. Amy Henry and Nick Warnock enjoyed each other's company and played off of each other in a flirtatious and lighthearted way.

So it was no surprise that Amy hit upon a scheme that everyone on the team agreed to. She proposed selling advertising and

Amy Henry proposed selling advertising attached to the backs and sides of the rickshaws during a competition in season one.

having posters printed to attach to the backs and sides of the rickshaws. Proceeds from the rides would never amount to much, but the sale of advertising could bring in the kind of money needed to win the competition. The team capitalized on connections to people they'd worked with on previous tasks, like Marquis Jet and Donny Deutsch's advertising firm. During the boardroom session, when the team discussed the huge margin of their win, Donald Trump commended them for their clever ideas and thinking outside of the box.

> Whether that flash of imagination comes during a solitary walk, in a conversation with someone else, or from brainstorming with several others, it is a creative moment that propels us out of the realm of the ordinary.

Whether that flash of imagination comes during a solitary walk, in a conversation with someone else, or from brainstorming with several others, it is a creative moment that propels us out of the realm of the ordinary to the world of unknown possibilities. On an even larger scale, those countries that foster creativity and free-spirited thinking have cornered the market on rapid advances in technology. Japan, for instance, is a leader in manufacturing products thanks to its access to financial resources and inexpensive labor, but its economy lags behind many other countries because the Japanese haven't encouraged the high level of innovation that has predominated in the United States. Economists who have studied this phenomenon note that Japanese culture emphasizes obedience, conformity, and compliance. Parents save money to educate their children in mathematics and the sciences, and it is in these fields that they excel. An interesting correlation is that the Japanese have an unusually high rate of depression and dissatisfaction with the quality of their lives. When we stifle our natural inclinations, the frustration shows up, not just in the economy but also in the way we feel.

Being Creative Means Taking Risks

In the classic 1970s film *Harold and Maude*, Ruth Gordon plays Maude, an eighty-year-old woman who befriends a fatalistic young college student who is fascinated with death. All but invisible to his socialite parents and the servants in their opulent mansion, Harold takes his greatest pleasure in life in faking his own death. In the opening scene he is dangling from a noose, legs midair, his head limp to one side. As his mother walks by she barely notices, snapping, "Harold, get down from there!" Obediently stepping down, he begins plotting his next stunt: drowning in the bathtub. In confidence, he tells his friend Maude that he rather enjoyed being dead, to which she replies, "A lot of people enjoy being dead, but they're not dead really; they're just backing away from life. Reach out, take a chance, and get hurt even. Play as well as you can. . . . Otherwise you've got nothing to talk about in the locker room."[4]

In his book *Jump In!*, Mark Burnett writes about a period in his life when he owned a successful marketing company, but all the time he felt that something was missing.[5] Not one to back away from life, he realized, after overhearing a producer at a Hollywood party talking about his projects, that what was missing was creativity. He knew he had to take more risks, and soon after he brought the nation a type of television programming that had never been done on such a grand, cinematic scale.

Being in the Zone

The difference between a career that stifles creative ideas and one that rewards innovation makes it clear: we need to satisfy our most basic and innate drive toward self-expression. Psychologist Abraham Maslow called it self-actualization, Sigmund Freud called it libido, athletic coaches call it "the zone," and now the buzzword is "flow."[6] Whatever you choose to call it, it can make the difference between trudging through a workday performing by rote or being intensely involved and passionate about your day's work.

> People get into "the zone" when they are totally absorbed in an activity; they lose their sense of time and feel great satisfaction with what they are doing.

People get into "the zone" when they are totally absorbed in an activity; they lose their sense of time and feel great satisfaction with what they are doing. The optimal setting for this feeling to occur is with a task that is challenging and when you get to apply your skills or talent. When too much of the day is spent doing undemanding work, the result is boredom and apathy. You may not experience these moments of optimal challenge every hour of every workday, but let's hope that at least some of the tasks required in your chosen profession provide some sense of flow.

The idea of flow was first suggested by a professor of social science at the Peter Drucker School of Business at Claremont University, Mihaly Csikszentmihalyi (pronounced chick-sent-me-high-ee).[7] His life's work has been to study what makes people truly happy, fulfilled, and satisfied. As a child in post-WWII Budapest, Hungary, he saw his country crumble under Stalin's oppressive rule. As members of the aristocracy, his family lost their social standing and most of their possessions. Many adults he knew there "disintegrated" when they realized their losses, but he was more interested in those who rose above those losses, who found a way to reinvent themselves.

Csikszentmihalyi was curious to know how some people live their lives like works of art and others are buffeted by adversity.[8] In his research, he surveyed 250,000 people in several countries about what made them happy. He began with artists, who described being in an "ecstatic state" when they were creating something with their own hands. Some of the painters he interviewed told of becoming so involved in the artistic process that they forgot to eat and would never tire. They often mentioned achieving a state of euphoria. Their description of this positive mood illustrates the role that creativity plays in our lives. Being happy and optimistic fuels a broad, expansive state of mind, and in turn, creativity brings about a sense of happiness, sometimes even euphoria.

> Being happy and optimistic fuels a broad, expansive state of mind, and in turn, creativity brings about a sense of happiness, sometimes even euphoria.

In addition to describing the zone that people reach when they are highly absorbed in a task, Mihaly Csikszentmihalyi also discovered that a life full of joy is a condition that people purposefully cultivate and willfully choose.[9]

Just as it is possible to change your degree of optimism by selecting how you explain the events of your life, it is possible to choose more creative experiences in the course of the day. This choice can be as simple as challenging the policies, procedures, and structures around you that may be stifling.

The idea that we can *choose* to be imaginative may seem a bit foreign because we often have the notion that inspiration strikes like a bolt of lightning or that we need to be visited in the middle of the night by a muse. One of my professors in a creative writing class once announced that there was a secret to great writing.

The whole class leaned forward, pencils midair, to record the secret. After a long, dramatic pause, he simply said, "Write." Simply put, the best way to tap into your inventiveness is to act: put pen to paper, sit at a potter's wheel, or whatever. Make the commitment; place value and importance on innovation and imagination, regardless of your work setting.

Today's companies aren't run assembly-line style by automatons who come and go, quietly punching the time clock, as in Chaplin's *Modern Times*. Our organizations are flesh-and-blood networks intricately woven from families, friends, and passions. Top companies to work for offer daycare and family leave as benefits. College graduates entering the workforce have choices in selecting an employer, and the leadership in a company that fosters a positive work setting is ahead of the pack, in more ways than one. Not only does a positive environment draw the best employees, it also fuels the innovation that's necessary to stay ahead in a competitive world.

> Simply put, the best way to tap into your inventiveness is to act: put pen to paper, sit at a potter's wheel, or whatever.

Staying Ahead of Moore's Law

It is all well and good that optimism leads to more creativity and that creativity produces more positive emotions, but do optimism and creativity have any impact on actual productivity in an organization? Words like *innovation, creativity*, and *inventiveness* frequently appear in today's business journals and are topics in leadership seminars, but is this just a passing fad? It's easy to see the effects of ingenuity in the major deals drawn up by entrepreneurs. People like Donald Trump are skilled at dreaming up new opportunities to create wealth. His particular forte is real estate development, but originality is a driving force in nearly all sectors of business. Marketing and sales move industries forward so quickly that if companies don't come up with fresh ideas regularly, someone else will.

Moore's law states that the power and speed of integrated circuitry and technological development double every eighteen months. Moore's law is attributed to Gordon E. Moore, a cofounder of Intel who currently serves as chairman emeritus. He actually predicted that the rate of technological development would double every twenty-four months, but it has turned out to double every eighteen months, and most experts, including Moore, expect the law to hold for at least another two decades.[10] If a company hesitates, its competition will pass it by in a flash.

Innovation empowers those companies that stay in the lead with a winning combination of risk-taking and broad-minded thinking. Those maverick companies that knock the old-timers out of the saddle have done so with an up-to-the-minute perspective. They aren't weighed down by outdated rules and management practices. Indeed, both the old guard and the mavericks appreciate the need for highly resourceful and open-minded leadership. A leader has to cultivate an atmosphere of flexibility and expansive thinking throughout the organization. She should be agile enough to run with new trends and shifting needs. In fact, the most creative leadership has a knack for filling a void that the consumer wasn't even completely aware of. For example, back in 1983, when Chrysler introduced its 1984 model, a sporty-looking four-door van with folding seats, to shuttle the kids back and forth, they did it before the parents in the suburbs realized that's what was needed.[11]

> **Innovation empowers those companies that stay in the lead with a winning combination of risk-taking and broad-minded thinking.**

Likewise, entertainment-industry leader Ted Turner noticed that family life had changed quite a bit since the 1960s and 1970s, when folks used to gather around the TV set to watch the six o'clock evening news.[12] People wanted to get their daily dose of news, but at the standard news hour they were likely to be stuck in traffic, on the commuter train, watching Little League practice, or grabbing dinner at the drive-thru. At the same time, lighter, hand-held cameras made it easier for TV journalists to capture a developing story. In what Carl Jung called synchronicity, Turner also anticipated our boredom with tired old sitcoms and our new fascination with hard-edged reality. Like any artist, he wove together these bits and pieces of his medium into a brand-new design of round-the-clock news coverage. The major networks were too bogged down in tradition and convention to see that the tide had changed and CNN slipped into the marketplace to become the leading news program with its fresh format and gritty coverage.

It isn't just the start-up companies that thrive on creativity. Being responsive to customers and coming up with innovative products has been a way of life at 3M for more than a century. The company was founded on the principle that employees need the freedom to take risks and be encouraged and rewarded for new ideas. The result has been a steady stream of products— over 50,000 innovations to date.[13] Much of this pioneering spirit at 3M comes from the ideology of its former president and chairman of the board, William L. McKnight. McKnight believed that "management that is destructively critical when mistakes are made kills initiative. It's essential that we have many people with initiative if we are to continue to grow." He made 3M a place where ideas proliferate, in an environment where imagination and cooperation are enthusiastically embraced. It is this atmosphere that continues to make 3M a leader in the industry.

> Creativity flourishes in an atmosphere that explicitly rewards attempts as well as successes.

The 3M story is a reminder that people have to be encouraged to believe in their abilities, even after repeated failures. Creativity flourishes in an atmosphere that explicitly rewards attempts as well as successes. The people who make up the bulk of an organization have to feel comfortable failing before they can take the riskier, more creative approach. Encouraging attempts instead of successes builds people's confidence and self-esteem, and we know that positive feelings add fuel to people's creative abilities.

Those at the top have to be free to make mistakes as well, and at that level you can't be controlled by fear. It was a huge gamble in 1995 for Charles Schwab's senior management to take the lead in online trading rather than sit back until all the kinks got worked out.[14] By placing itself on the front line, the company took a significant risk in the vast unknown world of the Internet. Because of its gutsy decision, the Charles Schwab organization has now established itself as a leader in online trading. Years ago, the slow-moving steel or textile industries could pass on time-tested operations for generations, but that inward approach today would leave a business paralyzed. Business leaders now have to hop quickly to the next lily pad to find a new strategy, and they have to do so without doubt or hesitation.

The Creative Leader

One of the most important tasks a leader has is to find the creativity killers in his organization and eliminate them. Trump credits a great deal of his success to being able to "play it loose."[15] In *The Art of the Deal*, he notes that too much structure kills imagination and the ability to be entrepreneurial. If you truly believe, as Abraham Maslow did, that we are all striving to better ourselves and to fulfill our human potential, then creativity is a compelling inner drive in all of us that seeks expression. When business consultant Peter Drucker spoke to a panel of senior-level executives, he asked them to raise their hands if there was a lot of dead wood in their company. When most of them raised their hands he asked, "Were the people dead wood when you interviewed them and decided to hire them, or did they become dead wood?"[16] Although it may not be their intention, many organizations manufacture a lot of dead wood.

An illustrative story is that of the U.S. Forest Service and its suggestion system. If employees wanted to suggest a new service, how to streamline a process, or make some type of improvement, they had to fill out a punishing four-page suggestion form. In one region with over 2,500 employees, only 252 suggestions were made over a four-year period—or one idea per person every forty years. Then the Forest Service streamlined the procedure so that a brief description could be submitted over e-mail and in the first year they received over 6,000 suggestions.[17]

The creative leader can't be threatened by sharing the task of innovation and in fact should try to unlock ideas from every layer of the company. Richard Branson, head of Virgin Enterprises, gives each of his employees his phone number. If they want to pitch an idea, they simply call him. That's how a Virgin Airlines flight attendant started up a wedding planning boutique called Virgin Bride.[18] She was having so much trouble planning her own wedding that she saw a need to be met—and so did her boss!

> **The creative leader can't be threatened by sharing the task of innovation and in fact should try to unlock ideas from every layer of the company.**

Reducing the creativity killers by streamlining and generously accepting employees' ideas, whether successful or not, is a great start for the emerging leader. An even better place to begin is to take a conscientious and objective look at how you approach your own work. Are you sitting on the bench or are you out there taking risks? When an executive faces a crisis such as stagnation, boredom, or crippling fear, he may turn to an "executive coach" to get through it. Years of stifled self-expression, playing it close to the chest, and avoiding all risks can result in a good deal of ennui. Playing it safe will keep you out of harm's way, and maybe even gets the kids through college, but it can also petrify your career. Describing the thrill of taking risks, Winston Churchill said, "Nothing in life is so exhilarating as to be shot at without results."[19]

Creativity and originality are intimately connected to a tolerance for ambiguity and unpredictability, to comfort with a lack of structure or loss of control, and to the ability to be spontaneous and go forward without a plan. Creativity results when we give full attention to the present moment and briefly let go of the future. Contrast that with a stranglehold on obsessive planning, a compulsive need for structure, and a general fear of the unknown. At the heart of a reliance on organization and structure is a lack of self-confidence and fear of the unknown. There is a simple test you can take to gauge your degree of spontaneity and your willingness to improvise. When next speaking to a colleague or friend, pay attention to what you are doing in the middle of the conversation. Are you planning what to say next, mentally rehearsing your reply, or are you fully engaged and absorbed in what this person has to say? Most of us could use practice in listening better, planning less, and trusting our ability to think on our feet.

> We create rules and restrictions so that we can carefully prepare for every contingency, but in reality, there is no way to completely anticipate everything that may cross our paths.

Like the main character played by Tom Cruise in *Risky Business*, we are compelled to plan in some way for the future, when sometimes the best thing we can do is just to let go (although the term used in the movie was much more colorful). We create rules and restrictions so that we can carefully prepare for every contingency, but in reality, there is no way to completely anticipate everything that may cross our paths. Of course it's nice to have a certain amount of predictability, control, and order in business, but the wise leader guards against inflexibility, rigidity, or fear of the unknown.

Creative people are drawn to the mystery of the unknown and they become more focused, more alert, and more interested when a monkey wrench is thrown into their plans. The person in that state of flow, or who is self-actualized, is so absorbed in the present that she doesn't see problems as foreign—they are just part of the task. That optimal state of being in the zone can be difficult and challenging, however. It's much easier to stick with the predictable and the structured. But the rewards of creativity are fine compensation for the efforts involved. In summary, creativity is fueled by a healthy self-confidence, self-respect, and an expectation that you will be able to deal with those things outside your control. The environment is seen as a trustworthy place, not full of danger. There's a calm assuredness that you can rise to meet the ever-changing requirements of your situation. Freedom from anxiety and doubt fuels your optimistic belief that setbacks are only temporary and not to be taken personally. When you look to the future, it is not monstrous or frightening and therefore you feel no need to prepare for all contingencies; you trust yourself to know what to do when the time comes. Such positive expectations about yourself are contagious, and as a leader, you can spread those feelings easily throughout the organization.

> Self-confidence, enthusiasm, optimism, and creativity are all woven together in the fabric that shapes the most inspiring leaders.

Self-confidence, enthusiasm, optimism, and creativity are all woven together in the fabric that shapes the most inspiring leaders. The contestants on *The Apprentice* embody so many of these traits that their success is virtually guaranteed. If you feel you could use a little help in being more spontaneous, flexible, and creative, here are some ways to start.

The Guide for Creative Leadership

Initial Steps

The single most important thing you can do to develop your creative ability is to stay hopeful. The correlation between positive mood and expansive thinking is well documented. So, review the exercises at the end of Chapter 2. Next, size up your surroundings and find ways to change them that will enhance your ability to be creative. Listed below are just a few ideas:

- **Check your surroundings**. Look for the little things that are draining your liveliness and sapping your enthusiasm. Watch out for the following energy zappers:

Clutter in your office and at home

Depressing furnishings

Distractions

- **Eliminate the clutter**. Piles of unfinished paperwork, unopened mail, and past-due projects glare in defiance every time you walk by. Clutter can affect how you feel, including how stressed you are. Set aside a weekend to attack that clutter. Be merciless. Clean your closets of old clothes you no longer wear; sort through piles of paperwork and projects that have been languishing.

- **Create comfortable surroundings**. Check the lighting in your home and office and consider getting full-spectrum light bulbs, which may provide additional sunlight. Add plants, pictures, candles, a stereo, or a bubbling fountain, if these will lift your spirits.

- **Eliminate distractions**. Who's really in charge here? Have you let your cell phone or laptop become your task-master? Hang out the "Do Not Disturb" sign and turn off the phone. Instead of checking e-mail and voicemail throughout the day, set specific times once or twice each day. Warning: Excessively checking your e-mail and voicemail may be a sign of Internet addiction. It could take a while to break this routine, and you may relapse occasionally before you kick the habit.

Further Steps

- **Make a list of activities that you find challenging**. Brainstorm for additional activities to investigate but don't worry about finding the right ones immediately. You want your list to be long and comprehensive before you settle in on particular activities. Here are some ideas:

Songwriting, guitar, piano

Ceramics, pottery-making

Golf, tennis, softball, hiking, rollerblading, mountain climbing, volleyball

Swimming, surfing, scuba diving

Chess, bridge

Knitting, needlepoint, weaving

Woodworking, watercolor painting, sculpture

Search the list for activities you are drawn to. You may like an activity you are naturally talented in, such as singing, or it may be something that you haven't tried in a long time, such as softball. It could even be something brand-new that you've secretly wanted to try for quite some time, like tango dancing.

- **Learn a skill that will help you experience flow**. Take a look at that list of activities that you find interesting. Remember, those activities that put you in the zone will be challenging ones where some skill is required—even if it is a new skill you will acquire. Perhaps your list included rollerblading, mountain climbing, or scuba diving. Check with your local YMCA for scuba classes; some cities offer Learning Annex classes for activities like rollerblading. And there are many books about mountain climbing, and local outdoor-equipment stores such as REI often offer classes.

- **Practice makes perfect**. As counterintuitive as it might sound, inventiveness and spontaneity need to be practiced to come more easily. Books with wonderful exercises to spark creativity include *The Artist's Way* and *Writing Down the Bones*.[20] For example, in *The Artist's Way*, an exercise called "The Morning Pages" suggests writing a three-page journal entry each day.[21] Getting into daily habits like journaling will help get your creative juices flowing.

* **Write for 30 minutes**. Put the pencil to the page, keep your hand moving, and see what comes forth. Don't edit yourself and don't worry about spelling or grammar. Writing down your thoughts will help crystallize them. Some ideas to help you get started:

  Your first memory

  A favorite moment

  Your favorite color

  The street you live on

Going Beyond

If you are like most of the contestants on *The Apprentice*, you are probably too vivacious and energetic to have much patience for uncovering deep psychological meanings; you just want to get to the point! However, if you try some of the above suggestions and your creativity is still blocked or you feel you still can't take risks, you may be a victim of some old, outdated fears instilled when you were young.

Sometimes, childhood admonishments for our "own protection" become sour reminders in our heads. All of those cautions, warnings, and reprimands take up residence and make judgments about our every move. They form our worries: fear of making mistakes, fear of being noticed, fear of taking chances. If you are too concerned about playing it safe, break the habit by examining your fears.

For each fear that you uncover, ask yourself where it might have come from. For instance a fear of failure could be traced to a family who expected perfection. Although some good may have come from such standards (such as a solid work ethic) you can challenge those old notions that are now more restricting than helpful. Recognize that although your family members may have been well-meaning, *they* may not have always known best. Challenge your fear by questioning those outdated beliefs. *Was there ever a time when you weren't perfect? How did it turn out? Did you recover? Would you expect your own child to always be perfect? Would you lose respect for a friend if she made a mistake? What is the worst thing that could happen if you make a mistake?*

Once you recognize the faulty logic behind your fear you can begin to change your old habits; the best way to do that is to create new habits. Develop the habit of questioning your fears, rather than following them blindly. Write down your fear and then rewrite it with some more reasonable modifications. For example, the fear *"I may not succeed"* can be modified to: *"I may not succeed right away but I can try again. The only way I can completely fail is if I don't try."*

As with any habit you try to break, it takes patience. You can expect that the first few times you take a risk, the old fears will act up, but you can be rid of them eventually. You'll start to evict those unwelcome worries one by one, so that you'll have room for flexibility and imagination.

CHAPTER FOUR

Resilience: Jumping the Hurdles

The leaders I met, whatever walk of life they were from, whatever institutions they were presiding over, always referred back to the same failure: something that happened to them that was personally difficult, even traumatic, something that made them feel that desperate sense of hitting bottom—as something they thought was almost a necessity. It's as if at that moment the iron entered their soul; that moment created the resilience that leaders need.

> —WARREN G. BENNIS, lecturer, theorist on leadership, and author
> of *Leaders*, named by the *Financial Times* as one of the best
> business books of all times

RESILIENCE IS THE HALLMARK of the entrepreneurial spirit. The true test of the innovator is what you do after the door is slammed in your face. Donald Trump likes to tell the story about walking down the street with Marla Maples and seeing a homeless man curled up on the front stoop of a house. He turned to her and said "That man has more money than I do." He was referring to his very public meteoric fall from financial fame to bankruptcy.

In the mid-eighties, Donald Trump was several billion dollars in debt. He attributed his losses to his own complacency, as well as to the Tax Reform Act of 1986. His rather tongue-in-cheek comeback stories range from playing golf to having a prenuptial agreement, but it was probably his hard work, skillful negotiating, and unsinkable belief in himself that brought him back to the top. The end of the 1980s were lean years for Donald Trump, but in what he calls the "Great Depression of 1990," he renegotiated millions of dollars in bank loans, built a wildly successful casino in Atlantic City, outmaneuvered one of South America's richest men for rights to the Miss Universe pageant, and broke ground on a development project in New York City that would prove to be extremely lucrative.

Trump's three casinos—the Taj Mahal, Castle, and Plaza—ended up in Chapter 11 in 1992, after a recession that began the previous year. His determined climb out of personal bankruptcy and back to billionaire status is detailed in his 1997 book *The Art of the Comeback*. His story has all the markings of a man with true resilience: he was able to find the humor even at the lowest point, including seeing the irony of a homeless person having more money than he had. Today, Donald Trump is an icon of success in the business world.

> The optimistic person might overestimate his control of a situation, but that outlook nevertheless achieves positive results.

His unique brand of resilience is composed of relentless determination and what some would say is an overinflated belief in himself. As was true with optimism, discussed in Chapter 1, a person's positive emotions don't have to be grounded in reality to exert a positive effect. The optimistic person might overestimate his control of a situation, but that outlook nevertheless achieves positive results. Quite the contrary, the resilient person insists on self-efficacy, even when reality might tell a different story.

Ultimately, what matters is that a person who believes in her own capabilities is more likely to keep trying and eventually succeed. There are always the red flags of realism, uncertainty, and fear. The pessimistic, cautious person may have garnered some success in the past, but in a world where change and innovation are the standard, resilience, and its cousin adaptability, are necessary to survive and succeed.

It takes flexibility and adaptability to hold the attention of a capricious public looking for the next big thing. In the 1990s, the Apple Computer was in decline as its competitor Microsoft introduced the Windows operating software.[1] It wasn't until Steve Jobs, Apple's illustrious cofounder, came back in 1997 that the company began to revive. Jobs had made a career of being tenacious in an industry driven by rapid change; he's been able to continually find fertile ground for new ideas. When he came back to Apple, he correctly judged the climate and put the company back on top with his venture into iPod and iTunes; filling a niche that had been occupied by illegal downloading sites. Once again, Jobs made his way back to the top.

> That special ability to look for alternatives and new applications is what propels the resilient person through hard times.

To a successful person, there is nothing as attractive as the computer not yet designed, the system to be created, the song to be written. Stability and predictability are not the least bit appealing to someone of this ilk; actually, an entrepreneur is stifled by convention and rules, as we discussed in Chapter 3. That special ability to look for alternatives and new applications is what propels the resilient person through hard times. The question isn't if you will get thrown for a loop, it's when you will. The people who can't quickly adapt are doomed; those who believe that adversity points the way to opportunity will thrive.

Ordinary Magic

After the Twin Towers of the World Trade Center were hit and toppled, a small part of us fell like dominoes across the country. We looked at each other in dismay, slept fitfully, and barely managed to drag ourselves to work in the following days. How could we ever feel safe again in our country and our homes? How could we move forward when we couldn't even comprehend the number of lives lost or bear the force of so much grief? Slowly, small pieces of the tragedy registered in our brains—a name here, a family photo there, a friend or boss or family member remembering a loved one.

There was a feeling of helplessness, a feeling that we could do nothing to assist. Blood donations sat in containers, unused; hospital staff and emergency personnel rushed to give assistance, only to sit idly by, watching the scene unfold on television with the rest of us. Since the tragedy, the weeks and months have turned into years and it has become a part of who we are. In remembering lost colleagues and friends, we recall the smoke and the sorrow, but also the strength shown by Mayor Rudy Giuliani, the flag flying above ground zero, and our capacity to love and care for each other. We are resilient; we will come back.

Resilience is ordinary magic.[2] Our capacity to withstand tragedy is both extraordinary and commonplace. The course of anyone's lifetime is bound to be touched by loss, although rarely is it of the magnitude of 9/11. A life well lived, a life lived not dictated by fear, has inevitable losses on a personal level, and the way we respond determines whether we are left feeling hopeless and bitter, never to trust again, or whether we jump right back into the swirling current. The magical quality of resilience is that it is more than just "surviving" a crisis; it is the alchemy of turning a setback into an advancement.

Thankfully, disaster isn't something we often face, so coping well seems a rare and extraordinary act of heroism. Disasters like 9/11 have taught us otherwise. Following the terrorist attacks, it was estimated that only about 7 percent of the residents of Manhattan experienced symptoms of post-traumatic stress disorder (PTSD), and that figure dropped to less than 2 percent after four months. In the aftermath of the Oklahoma City bombing, the body handlers showed "remarkable resilience," requiring very little in the way of grief counseling.[3] Indeed, we marvel at the bravery of people who respond to disasters with such fortitude, but the bigger picture shows resiliency as one of our shared human virtues. In the overall population, as opposed to those who come to clinics seeking treatment, effective coping is far more common than previously thought.

> **Resilience isn't the absence of sadness and hurt; it's just that those who are more agile at coping can recover quickly while others tumble down into despair.**

In northern U.S. forests, when the conifers die, they open up the area to more light and thus create the right environment for aspen and birch trees to grow; this is called forest secession, and it reflects a healthy ecosystem. Scientists have labeled these ecosystems "resilient." Similarly, one of our finer qualities as people is the skill we have for rallying hope and faith in the very darkest moments. Those who are the most resilient are able to climb back up into the light by securing their footing in a series of slow, steady rises. Resilience isn't the absence of sadness and hurt; it's just that those who are more agile at coping can recover quickly while others tumble down into despair. In an effort to understand more about coping and thriving under bad conditions, researchers have conducted studies to pinpoint the qualities that help some people be more nimble than others in recovering from adversity.

By coincidence, one such study of resilience among students at the University of Michigan was finished just months before 9/11. After the tragedy, researchers conducted several follow-up interviews. To place the timing in perspective, the follow-up questionnaire was administered during the month following the 9/11 attack, when news reports were covering the five mysterious deaths from anthrax and there were the first U.S. and allied forces' air strikes against Afghanistan.

Those who took part in the study were candid about their fears of flying, about fears of future terrorist attacks, and about the possibility of war. They acknowledged anger, sadness, fear, disgust, and contempt, but also gratitude, love, joy, hope, and pride. Those who were rated as more resilient in the first study expressed more positive emotions, a better overall mood, and renewed faith, friendship, and love in the follow-up. They appeared to be able to bounce back even more satisfied with life and more optimistic than before. They were deeply saddened and moved by the effects of the terrorist attacks, but they did not feel overwhelmed, and negative experiences were offset by positive ones. They showed resilience, with the ability to withstand the uncomfortable feelings of grief and loss and then move on with renewed appreciation and resolve.[4] (It will be interesting to hear the tales of resilience that are certain to emerge from the events of Hurricane Katrina as well.)

> Those who were rated as more resilient in the first study expressed more positive emotions, a better overall mood, and renewed faith, friendship, and love in the follow-up.

Even recently, popular thinking was that, with enough setbacks, losses, and traumas early in life, people would develop mental illness or turn to drugs and alcohol. But we know now that psychological resilience is a relatively stable personality trait characterized by the ability to bounce back from negative experiences and be flexible while adapting to the ever-changing demands of life. This was something that psychologists accidentally stumbled upon in the pursuit of understanding depression and how it is we "learn" to be hopeless and helpless.

Tales of scientific discoveries are full of accidental findings and stumbles onto important facts while looking for something completely different. Such moments of serendipity are not purely blind luck; there is an element of opportunism in the venture as well. "Accidental" good fortune is a close cousin to resilience because perseverance leads, eventually, to success. The English writer Horace Walpole coined the term *serendipity* from an ancient Persian story titled "Peregrinations of the Three Sons of the King of Serendip."[5]

The King recognized that, although his sons were quite well educated, life experience is what seasons a truly great leader. He sent his sons out into the world without servants, money, or horses. In the course of their adventures they turned misfortune into gold, and in the tradition of happy endings, each one married and became emperor of a kingdom.

The Dogs That Wouldn't Lie Down

The relationship between fortunate findings and resilience can also be found in science. It is by pure serendipity that the man who illustrated the "inevitable" nature of "learned helplessness" instead learned about resilience and is now a leader in the field of positive psychology. The learned helplessness study is solidly imprinted on every young psychology student and is sure to show up on a midterm or a final.[6]

In 1965, Martin Seligman joined the University of Pennsylvania's psychology department, which was conducting a study of learning. The original study was meant to be a Pavlovian-type experiment in which dogs were to be exposed to a high-pitched tone, followed by a mild shock. It was predicted that the dogs would come to associate the tone with the shock so that later, even in the absence of the shock, they would react to the tone with the same fear. After the pairing had produced the desired association, the dogs were placed in a large box with two compartments separated by a low wall. An electrical current could be activated on the floor on either side of the box, and when the dog felt the shock, it simply had to jump to the other side.

Normally, dogs and other animals learn this escape behavior very quickly, but, in this case, the dogs weren't trying to escape; they just lay down and gave up. Seligman quickly recognized that something much more important than simple conditioning had taken place. The dogs had "learned" that the shock was unavoidable in the first box; therefore, they learned that it was hopeless to try to escape and they didn't even try.

Seligman and a fellow student, Steven Maier, abandoned their first experiment to test this more interesting hypothesis: Could dogs learn that a situation was hopeless? They divided twenty-four dogs into three groups of eight and exposed the first eight to a shock from which they could escape. The second group was exposed to identical shocks from which there was no escape, and the third group received no shocks at all. The next day they put the dogs in the box and gave them shocks that they could easily escape from by jumping over the partition.

The results were amazing! Within seconds the dogs that had controlled the shocks and the dogs that didn't receive any shocks quickly jumped over the partition. But six of the eight dogs that had learned that nothing they did mattered just gave up and lay down, even though they could see the partition and the other side of the box. For the group that had no control over the shock in the first part of the experiment, there was no incentive to escape. They had, as Seligman and Maier had predicted, *learned* to be helpless.

The study had far-reaching implications in explaining why humans get depressed and feel hopeless. Both the helpless dog and the depressed person have learned from past experiences that their actions are useless. In both situations, they simply give up hope that their behavior can make a change for the better. For instance, a child in a crowded orphanage will soon learn that crying does not bring the comfort of being held because the workers are too busy. Eventually the child becomes apathetic and withdrawn, and won't bother crying anymore. It will just lie down in its crib and give up. Similarly, seniors in nursing homes who relinquish control over their day-to-day activities become more depressed and have poorer health than those who maintain a sense of personal power.

Seligman 's study was well received and became standard fare in colleges and universities. But what about those annoying dogs, the two in eight that quickly sprang to action and jumped over that partition despite having been in the situation where most dogs learned to be helpless? After many repetitions of the experiment, Seligman could no longer ignore those stubborn and persistent canines. The dogs that refused to give up seemed to have some innate sense of hopefulness that shielded them from learning to give up. When I first met *The Apprentice* candidates, I was instantly reminded of this study, and it seemed that many of them have that same inborn inclination to jump over the hurdles rather than give up or get depressed.

Hoping to replicate Seligman's study, other experimenters repeated the conditions with people, giving them insolvable problems or inescapable noise, but there were always some obstinate outliers who wouldn't give up. It seemed that the effects of the environment and the conditions involved in shaping helplessness could go only so far to explain the differences in reactions to unavoidable adversity.

> The first step in building resilience is to face a problem and ask the hard-hitting questions; the next is to start looking for alternatives.

A decade of this type of variability persuaded Seligman to ask the tough questions about the completeness of his learned helplessness theory and whether it was the slam-dunk cause-and-effect relationship the world of psychology had come to believe. As you will see in the section titled "The Guide for Resilient Leadership," the first step in building resilience is to face a problem and ask the hard-hitting questions; the next is to start looking for alternatives. In a case of life imitating science, Seligman's resilience paved the way for a revision of his study.[7] He had to ask, What is it about some people that imparts buffering strength, making them invulnerable to helplessness? What is it about other people that make them collapse at the first inkling of trouble?

Many of the tasks on *The Apprentice* give the candidates "insolvable" problems and impossible deadlines, and the majority of them don't get ruffled by the pressure; they actually seem to thrive on it. Is this something that the candidates learned in life, or is it some type of inborn trait? Because some of them have had pasts full of misfortune while others have had a pretty carefree life to this point, it would seem to suggest that there is a type of personality that is naturally more inclined to be hopeful in the face of setbacks.

The Giggle Twins

Answers to these questions can be found in the study of constitutional differences. It had been firmly established that there was a genetic component to anger and depression, but why would Mother Nature be exclusive to the more negative character traits? What if the roots of positive emotions like happiness, joy, and resilience also had a grounding in genetics?

To untangle all of the various influences that come into play when it comes to personality variables, researchers turned to twin studies in an attempt to answer that age-old nature/nurture question that always pops up. The short answer seems to be that, although personality traits have multiple influences, some traits have a stronger genetic component than others. Twin studies provide a natural laboratory setting that allows us to separate genetics and environment. There are preexisting conditions of a laboratory experiment with a group of identical twins sharing 100 percent of their genetic material and fraternal twins sharing 50 percent. Identical twins who share precisely the same genes and are raised together in the same family can be compared to those who, through adoption, grow up in different environments, thus teasing out the effects of environment and genetics.

If the twins have a similar personality trait regardless of whether they were raised in the same home, it is likely that the particular characteristic has a strong genetic influence. Dissimilarities in their character would make the case for the influence of their surroundings. Some of the most famous twin studies involved intelligence and demonstrated that IQ, for the most part, is inherited, although the environment does play a role by offering stimulation or deprivation.

An optimistic, resilient attitude comes largely under the influence of genetics. If one identical twin is cheery, hopeful, and bubbly, odds are that the other twin will have the same disposition, even if they grew up on opposite sides of the country. Although *The Apprentice* candidates' family histories do not constitute a controlled study, the candidates often relate that they are the only ones among their siblings to have an upbeat and resilient personality.

If you sift through the data points in those statistics and pluck out an individual pair of these doppelgangers, the argument for heredity comes to life. One of the most famous cases in the twin literature is that of the Giggle Twins, so named because of their tendency to erupt into laughter.[8] Barbara Herbert found her lost twin, Daphne Goodship, several decades ago. The women, now over sixty years old, are both pretty, slightly plump, and have short silver hair. They were separated and placed into two different British families when they were just babies, after their single mother killed herself.

> Although *The Apprentice* candidates' family histories do not constitute a controlled study, the candidates often relate that they are the only ones among their siblings to have an upbeat and resilient personality.

Their similarities were apparent from the first moment of their reunion. Both selected cream-colored dresses and brown velvet jackets to wear that day. They had both named their odd habit of crooking their little fingers and pushing up their nose with the palm of their hands "squidging." Both left school at the age of fourteen; both fell down the stairs when they were fifteen and consequently weakened their ankles. In choosing a career, both had elected to work in local government. They met their future husbands at age sixteen at a Town Hall dance, miscarried in the same month, then gave birth to two boys and a girl. They discovered that they were both squeamish about heights and the sight of blood, preferred to drink their coffee cold, and had tinted their hair auburn at one time.

Extensive psychological and medical research has been carried out on these two women, along with hundreds of sets of twins at the University of Minnesota's Center for Twin and Adoption Research. What the researchers have discovered is that there is a pervasive genetic influence across most of the physical and psychological domains that are tested.

The laundry list of shared similarities for separated identical twins makes you wonder if any aspect of your personality has ever come under your free will. Twin studies have intimated that everything from our political persuasion to our preferences in clothing is somehow related to the complex coding carried in our DNA.

> Twin studies have intimated that everything from our political persuasion to our preferences in clothing is somehow related to the complex coding carried in our DNA.

Although heritability wields a powerful influence, environmental influences still matter. Even height, which has a heritability of greater than 0.9 (1.00 being a perfect correlation), has increased quite dramatically in our own country and in countries like Japan, where dietary changes have occurred at a rapid pace. On average, most personality traits have a genetic influence of about 50 percent.[9] Both optimism and pessimism are greatly influenced by genes. Pessimism, however, appears to be a more stubborn personality trait that isn't quite as amenable to life's experiences—but that doesn't mean that, with effort, that type of attitude can't be changed. The tendency to be more or less optimistic is a preference, like being right-handed instead of left-handed. It doesn't mean that you can never learn to use the other hand.

Examined as a whole, the research indicates that those dogs that wouldn't lie down may have been the lucky recipients of genetic resilience. They were immune to their hopeless surroundings and didn't let it get them down. The same experiment illustrates that helplessness can be learned, and that the environment can "teach" those who are more susceptible that their efforts don't matter so they may as well just give up. By the same reasoning, it also means that even if you are susceptible and have succumbed to learned helplessness, you are also pliable enough to take a genetic predisposition and modify it through learning. What the learned helplessness studies teach us is that we do have a choice when faced with adversity. We can learn from the dogs that wouldn't lie down or the people who wouldn't give up when faced with an unsolvable problem.

Finding the Opportunity in the Problem

People who don't let setbacks or disappointments "stick" to them are the type of people who wouldn't have given up in the learned helplessness study. They somehow maintain a belief that sooner or later their efforts will bear fruit and they will find a way out of a difficult situation. Others who are less naturally resilient are more likely to give up and assume that there is no way to overcome or bounce back from the problem. They don't see that there really is a way to jump over the partition and get to the other side. However, in Seligman's experiments, when the researchers patiently taught the hopeless dogs a way out, they eventually learned to jump over the partition.

> In times of adversity, some will be naturally resilient with little guidance where some will give up, but even those who give up can learn to be more resilient.

So the model has a great deal to teach about handling adversity. In times of adversity, some will be naturally resilient with little guidance where some will give up, but even those who give up can learn to be more resilient. Each episode of *The Apprentice* is full of great examples of dealing with adversity and shows the difference it makes to maintain a positive attitude. You can learn not only how to get through a specific situation but also how to have a more resilient outlook overall.

Some people are extremely upbeat and flexible when faced

with any setback, some are bitterly disappointed and rigid about it, and others fall somewhere in the middle along the continuum. Extenuating circumstances factor in as well, and some people may be quite nimble at bouncing back from personal setbacks while work-related problems make them nuts. In the various seasons of *The Apprentice*, adversity is the name of the game, as contestants face insurmountable odds in trying to complete near-impossible tasks. The ways that they react to the difficulties are a direct measure for Donald Trump to use in his decision to fire someone.

We know that resilience is a combination of recognizing a problem and then finding a benefit in the situation. The contestants who were more capable of surmising the nature of a problem early and then finding some benefits or alternatives were visibly more successful at inspiring their teams and gaining consensus. More often than not, their ability to quickly adapt and alter their courses led to a win for their teams.

On *The Apprentice*, the tasks are extremely difficult and much more challenging than what would come up in a day-to-day business environment. For example, one task required that the teams renovate and rent an apartment in about one day. The time constraint made the prize worthwhile and made the show entertaining, but it also meant that the task was fraught with overwhelming obstacles that could quickly challenge a person's resilience. As with other tasks on the show, most *Apprentice* candidates rise to the challenge and come up with highly creative ways to overcome the obstacles in their way.

A Mental Rehearsal for Greater Resilience

While the research tells us that there is a strong genetic component to personality, it has just as vividly illustrated the power of the environment to shape inborn traits. For example, IQ, with one of the strongest genetic correlations, can still be raised or lowered depending on how stimulating the environment is at home and at school. Resilience can also be raised or lowered, and just as helplessness can be learned, so can tenacity.

You can practice ways of thinking that will make you more resilient and effective at handling upsets and setbacks. On the various tasks of *The Apprentice*, the project managers were much more likely to win the task and motivate their teams through really tough assignments if they practiced resilient ways of approaching problems. This required that they (1) recognize problems, (2) use mental rehearsal, and (3) find the benefits and alternatives in a problem.

> The project managers were much more likely to win the task and motivate their teams through really tough assignments if they practiced resilient ways of approaching problems.

Acknowledging and preparing for problems is a talent that can be developed and practiced, but for some people it requires a slight shift in perspective. Some folks are of the mind that acknowledging a problem is the first step in giving it power. One common belief is that if you pay attention to a problem, it will give it power and momentum, or that focusing on a problem will drain the motivation from a team.

But readiness to confront obstacles isn't a lack of optimism; it involves being prepared and confident that you will be capable of dealing with setbacks if and when you encounter them. First, however, you have to be willing to acknowledge that there is a problem. For example, during the rickshaw task in season one, the winning team took its time, brainstormed for a little longer than the opposition did, focused on the problem, and had an Aha! moment. The team realized that it would be difficult to profit from individual rides, as they were labor-intensive and couldn't cost that much, resulting in a low return. By grappling with the problem before hitting the streets and starting the task, the team realized what else it could do to generate revenue. During the brainstorming session team members wondered out loud if they could put advertising on their rickshaws. Before they sold a single ride to a customer, they were ahead of the game and won that particular task by a large margin.

People who are resilient are simply not intimidated by problems. It takes both patience and confidence to view setbacks as a challenge rather than a deterrent. In the previous example, the group patiently took the time to problem-solve before it even started. That willingness to accept problems as a natural part of a task is the foundation of resilience. Indeed, facing problems head-on prepares you for the setbacks and bumps in the road. A mental rehearsal is one of the most effective ways we have of preparing for problems and improving our skill and ability to perform at our peak.

> That willingness to accept problems as a natural part of a task is the foundation of resilience.

Athletes use mental rehearsal as a means of improving their performance in every sport ranging from golf to football. They vividly imagine the details of their competition and come up with contingencies for coping with setbacks. Mental imagery actually affects the physical aspects of their performance. In an interview with TV journalist Katie Couric, actor Christopher Reeve talked about his vivid dream life and how each night he dreamed of running, sailing, riding horses, and other favorite activities he had done before being paralyzed in a horseback riding accident. He was very pleased with his active and adventurous night life because, as the doctors had explained to him, when he dreamed, the muscles he used were actually stimulated and active.

Mental rehearsal works because the act of performing an activity in the imagination and achieving the desired outcome actually stimulates neural activity in the brain. These patterns become engraved in the brain and enable athletes to alter or enhance their performance by communicating information to the muscles. The same technique applies in mentally rehearsing for peak job-resilient performance. By imagining possible setbacks and successful solutions, you lay down the mental tracks of success, preparing both mind and body for a positive outcome when a problem arises.

Also, by mentally rehearsing for possible problems, you are inoculating yourself against the effects of learned helplessness. How is it that anticipating problems is productive when it sounds an awful lot like pessimism? The difference is simple: pessimism sees a problem as a stop sign and doesn't go anywhere after that; the person comes to a dead halt where there really is only a warning sign to slow down and try an alternate route.

> **By imagining possible setbacks and successful solutions, you lay down the mental tracks of success, preparing both mind and body for a positive outcome when a problem arises.**

When *The Apprentice* candidates were brainstorming for ideas on the rickshaw task, they were open-minded about the problems and rehearsed them in the privacy of the suite so that they were well prepared, but without generating some alternatives, they would never have won that task. A pessimist stops at the problem-finding stage; an optimist is able to look for and find the humor and benefit in a problem, which allows the individual to come up with alternatives.

> **A pessimist stops at the problem-finding stage; an optimist is able to look for and find the humor and benefit in a problem.**

Humor in the Face of Negativity

In both everyday business problems and in crisis, it is humor and hopefulness that lie at the heart of thriving in adversity. Chapter 3 highlighted the fact that positive emotions lead to more expansive, creative, and broadened thinking. Laughter and a sense of humor not only help lighten a serious situation and make us feel better but also set the stage for the kind of flexible thinking that helps alternatives surface.

In very tense situations that are often devoid of humor, we tend to be less efficient and more constricted in our responses. The relationship between efficiency and tension is an inverted U. At low levels of tension, there is a low level of efficiency, but at high levels of tension, there is also a low level of efficiency, and laughter helps us achieve that optimal level of productivity.

Humor, like optimism and the other positive emotions, can be cultivated in a group or team. What do you do when you have one or two people in the group who are negative and unproductive? How do you keep your sense of humor, stay resilient, and generate good alternatives when you are surrounded by people who take a negative approach to problems? It would be nice if there were some trick that could change people without their being aware of it, but people have a hard time changing, even when they want to do so.

Mental Martial Arts

You can't insist that other people change their negative outlook, but you can change how you react to them. One way to deal with opposition is simply to align with it.[10] If someone is hell-bent on being negative and you argue, the person will work harder to convince you he is right. If you agree and then redirect the conversation back to generating solutions, you can keep yourself resilient and keep the group motivated and moving along. As distasteful as it might seem to agree with someone who is detracting, aligning yourself with the opposition is the same principle as aikido, one of the ancient martial arts.[11] The philosophy of aikido is that you can neutralize opposition by blending with the energy of the attack and then using that

> The philosophy of aikido is that you can neutralize opposition by blending with the energy of the attack and then using that force against the assailant.

force against the assailant.[12] In essence, you employ nonresistance to redirect an attack back to the attacker in as smooth and humane way as possible.

The mental form of aikido works quite well to render a negative person helpless. By agreeing with his negative outlook, he no longer has to argue with you, so you have moved with the force of the attack. Then you make a more positive suggestion, change the subject, or simply bypass his involvement. For instance, you can say, "You know, you are right; this probably wouldn't work for you. Why don't we let someone else give it a try?" If you don't have the time or the patience to practice mental martial arts, or if the problem person keeps attacking, there are other methods to keep you and the rest of the group resilient in the face of all of this pessimism.

If the person you are dealing with is both negative *and* persistent (a deadly combination), you can give honest feedback, such as "Your complaining is distracting me, so please don't talk that way around me." An alternate solution is to have the negative person write down her list of complaints or worries. Sometimes the act of listing and writing down specifics helps her do something constructive with all of those fears.

Persevering in the Face of Adversity

It is hoped that you won't encounter too many negative situations in your work setting, but if you do, the three steps to resilience mentioned earlier in "A Mental Rehearsal for Greater Resilience" can help increase your ability to handle difficult people. First, recognize that there is a problem person in the group; second, mentally rehearse your response to the individual; and third, when you come up against a problem person, find the humor, the benefits, and the alternatives. By

> You can pretty accurately predict people's reactions to crises by examining their views of how much control they have over the situation.

practicing these skills you can tackle life's problems with flexibility and persistence.

There are also certain attitudes that increase the chance that you will persevere under adverse conditions. You can pretty accurately predict people's reactions to crises by examining their views of how much control they have over the situation. Researchers have called this self-efficacy. Self-efficacy is discussed in more detail in the next section.

People who believe they are at the whim of the fates or destiny are more likely to give up when difficulties strike them. If, however, they believe that they have control over their own destinies, they will keep going. These people bounce off the surface of a problem, shake off troubles, and charge right back. This process goes on until they either beat down the difficulty or find a small opening to squeeze right through.

A tenacious spirit colors a person's reactions to the major crises as well as the everyday setbacks and disappointments of life. During any given episode of *The Apprentice*, the contestants meet with plenty of both, and Sam Solovey from the first season encountered more than his fair share of setbacks. The core attitude that fuels his determinism is his belief that he has control over his own fate and that his actions will matter. Sam Solovey bounced back after nearly being fired in the first two boardrooms, and when he walked back for the third time, he still hadn't lost that spring in his step.

> **The same intensity that brings him success in business was too over-the-top for his teammates, but in the excitement that surrounded the show he couldn't temper his zeal.**

Looking back at the experience, Sam recognizes that the same intensity that brings him success in business was too over-the-top for his teammates, but in the excitement that surrounded the show he couldn't temper his zeal. The viewers disliked him at first, but just as he won over Donald Trump and his top advisers, he charmed his way into the hearts of the fans of the show. There was something irresistible in the way he valiantly fought during those boardrooms.

During the first boardroom, every member of the men's team said that, if they had to choose, they would have to let Sam go. They said he was too erratic and that his ideas were too distracting, but even as they offered up his name, most of them couldn't conceal their fondness for him. Behind closed doors, Donald, George, and Carolyn agreed that Sam had at least openly demonstrated his passion and warm heart. Sam stayed and another member of the team was fired, although the future looked quite bleak for Sam.

During the second boardroom, the men on the team again placed Sam's head on the chopping block, but his quirky tenacity intrigued Donald Trump, who hypothesized that he would either do "great things" or "bring a company to ruin." During that boardroom, Sam stood up and made a passionate speech drawing similarities between Trump's upbringing and his own. He did everything to express the intensity of his desire to work for the Trump organization. Producer Mark Burnett later described Sammy as a "lion" who sunk his claws into the mahogany table in the boardroom and wouldn't let go until they "plucked each nail out one by one." Sam was not giving up without a fight, and he was relatively unfazed that the rest of the team had turned on him.

In Sam's third, and last, episode, he was the project manager, and when the team lost, Donald Trump told him that it was finally time to go. Sam the lion let out a final roar, but reluctantly left the boardroom to join the two before him. In the fallout the day after his firing, the public was quick to criticize him and even delighted in his getting his long overdue walking papers. But as people got to know him they saw his tenacity and it won them over.

Sam has since appeared on programs with Oprah, David Letterman, and Howard Stern, and has also been mentioned in magazines and been in television spots with Donald Trump himself.

Although he was on *The Apprentice* for only three episodes, he is one of the most well-remembered contestants of that season, and his ability to keep popping back up after he'd been knocked down earned him an outpouring of public affection.

When patients in psychotherapy seek help for problems they're having in everyday life, it is often because they have resigned themselves to an "inescapable" fate. One ingredient of therapy is to learn how to change self-defeating attitudes and beliefs, especially those about having no control over outcomes. Someone who is resilient has a very different way of viewing upsets, and many of the contestants on *The Apprentice* have this resilient point of view.

> One ingredient of therapy is to learn how to change self-defeating attitudes and beliefs, especially those about having no control over outcomes.

For example, one candidate described seeing her younger brother die in a skiing accident, another had lost his ten-year-old daughter to cancer, and another worked in Manhattan and lost several dear friends in the World Trade Center attack. Unsolicited, they each wove the same pattern of hope and faith into their explanations of loss. Their worlds laced together heartbreak, anguish, remembrance, renewal, and joy. Although what happened to them was outside their control, they believe they can at least control their reactions.

A closely related form of resilience in the face of loss and tragedy is the ability to manage the disappointments and setbacks of everyday life. We all have varying degrees of tolerance for the way life pushes us back as we try to make our way forward. One reason the contestants on *The Apprentice* have garnered so many successes in business is that they don't take kindly to being bullied by life. They don't run away from a good fight; instead, they are selective listeners when someone says no. They stubbornly believe that they have control over their own fates and that eventually they can supplant any impediment.

Self-Efficacy and Self-Esteem

Perseverance and self-reliance figure prominently in good leadership. Albert Bandura, a social psychologist, called this characteristic "self-efficacy." Self-efficacy is the exact opposite of learned helplessness. It is the serum that inoculates children against poverty, drugs, low expectations, and abuse. When you try to tease apart the factors that explain why some children survive a harsh environment and don't learn to be helpless, you find that there are a few factors besides genetics that help people overcome the difficulties of their surroundings.

> Self-efficacy is the exact opposite of learned helplessness.

One primary factor is that resilient children have had at least one significant and involved adult in their lives, even in the absence of an intact family.[13] Adult involvement goes a long way toward increasing a child's sense of accomplishment; even a small amount of attention can do wonders to bolster a child's self-esteem. For example, Oprah Winfrey has spoken about a time when she was about nine years old. Though it was a fleeting interaction, she well remembers a politician's wife who was campaigning in her church one Sunday. The woman came over to say, "You are as pretty as a speckled pup." For the first time in her life, Oprah says she believed she was beautiful, and she never forgot that moment of kindness.

> Adult involvement goes a long way toward increasing a child's sense of accomplishment; even a small amount of attention can do wonders to bolster a child's self-esteem.

Just as central a factor for children to survive a harsh environment is a sense of personal power and a belief that they are capable of exercising control over their environment. Perhaps one of the most important things adult involvement can do is model this positive self-belief in personal power. Sharing a difficult experience with a child and explaining how you got through it can model that personal power for her.

So, too, can giving a child some choices so that she can exercise her own influence.

A third factor is adult attention. There is no doubt that adult attention goes a long way in shielding a child from the adversities of life, but it is interesting that many of our "supernormal" *Apprentice* contestants have an inborn ability to bounce back regardless of family dynamic. They are so flexible and adaptable that they seek out those positive relationships for themselves. For instance, one of the applicants was raised by a single parent who had to work long hours to keep up the house payments. The family lived in a nice neighborhood, but there was no one home for most of the day. In this family of three, one of the siblings got into quite a bit of trouble, but the one who applied to the show was resilient and personable; turns out, he spent all of his spare time next door, where there was a stay-at-home mom and a big family. He enjoyed the attention, the family involvement, and especially the home-cooked meals, making the most out of the situation at hand.

Sam Solovey had that same determination to seek out mentors and relationships. He relentlessly pursued—and eventually won over—Donald Trump and his advisers. What sets Sam apart is his insistence that he will clear the hurdles and eventually persevere. Sam has an inborn tenacity and is lucky enough to have both self-esteem *and* self-efficacy. The difference between the two is that self-esteem is a judgment about self-worth, whereas self-efficacy is a judgment about capability.

The Power of Underlying Beliefs

Self-efficacy is the fuel for resilience, and psychologists believe that it forms through experiences and feedback from others. The good news is that even if you have developed unproductive beliefs about how capable you are, beliefs can be changed. Regardless of where you were born on the resilience spectrum, the belief you have about your capabilities will affect how you think, feel, and behave in a given situation, owing to the expectations you have

What sets Sam Solovey apart is his insistence that he will clear the hurdles and eventually persevere.

about the outcome. Your beliefs about how much control you think you have derives from how much importance you give to your own effort and your ability versus luck or unknown factors. If you have confidence in your capability, you will give the effort your all, but you will feel powerless if you give more weight to chance or luck.

> **Regardless of where you were born on the resilience spectrum, the belief you have about your capabilities will affect how you think, feel, and behave in a given situation.**

Your beliefs not only affect how you think and feel, they also affect the outcome of a situation. The great tenor Enrico Caruso used to get crippling stage fright that interfered with his ability to perform, even though he was one of the most talented tenors of all time. As Albert Bandura noted, "Insidious self-doubts can easily overrule the best of skills." On the other hand, insidious self-assuredness is contagious and can compensate for a lack of experience. In Sam's case, he truly believed that he and Donald

Trump had a great deal in common, and that Trump would recognize his exceptional qualities if he just had the chance. In the boardroom, his belief that he was capable and that he could win led to his valiant fight to stay another week. Even when every other team member said he should be fired, it didn't affect Sam's opinion of himself.

> As Albert Bandura noted, "Insidious self-doubts can easily overrule the best of skills." On the other hand, insidious self-assuredness is contagious and can compensate for a lack of experience.

It could easily have gone the other way. If Sam had felt defeated, he probably would have behaved differently as a result. He might not have fought so passionately or had the courage to stand up and plead his case. Donald Trump would have smelled his defeated attitude like blood in the water.

As it was, even with his whole team against him, Sam managed to stay for three episodes and convince his mentor that he might be able to "do great things."

If you suspect that you have some self-defeating beliefs that are affecting your resilience, the next section of this chapter, "The Guide for Resilient Leadership," has some suggestions for modifying those destructive beliefs. You can learn what Sam already knows: that with the belief that persistence will pay off, you will eventually reach your goal.

Resilience is what tips the balance in favor of people's overcoming trauma and loss, as well as coping with everyday stresses and setbacks in the workplace. Sam did indeed learn from the best; his idol, Donald Trump, had his own share of adversity that was followed by a renewed and revitalized career. The greatest leaders embrace their times of adversity as the catalyst for even greater achievements and successes.

The Guide for Resilient Leadership

Initial Steps

There are four aspects of resilience at the heart of overcoming both personal and professional setbacks. The next time you encounter a problem, spend some time breaking it down into manageable parts:

Quickly recognize that there is a problem.

Find the humor, the benefit, or the alternative.

Adapt quickly—change course.

Retain or regain your self-confidence.

Tackle each one in the following ways:

- **Recognize the problem,** realizing that a problem-oriented outlook isn't pessimistic; it is what prepares you for those inevitable setbacks. Steven Jobs's focus on the problem of pirating of songs from the Internet led to the next big thing for Apple, the iPod.

- **Mentally rehearse**. At the beginning of any venture, envision and rehearse all of the possible pitfalls. Use the valuable tool of mental rehearsal that athletes use to help improve performance and prepare for any challenges that might come up. Imagine a task as vividly as possible and use your imagination to anticipate problems.

- **Find an alternative** and you may be surprised that the crisis has led to some real benefits. This is the way that resilient leaders spin straw into gold.

- **Use humor.** Finding alternatives requires a deep respect for imagination and creativity. Humor and positive emotions lead to more creative and expansive thinking. By keeping a positive attitude, you set the mood and lay the groundwork for new and inventive alternatives.

- **Adapt quickly.** Tap into a powerful law of nature. Those species of plants and animals that modify their patterns as fast as the environment changes are resilient and have hit the evolutionary jackpot. The key to adaptability is having a wide repertoire of responses.[14] Sometimes it pays to be silly, sometimes serious; sometimes strong, other times vulnerable; sometimes masculine, other times feminine. Emotional and behavioral flexibility results from having a variety of resources.

- **Counterbalance your efforts.** It takes practice, but the effort you put into developing your weaker sides, like working a muscle, will eventually lead to more flexible strength. The next time you run into a problem, make an honest list of the skills you've used. Take time to think how you could do it differently—it may be that what is required is the exact opposite of your natural tendency. Say you come up with the following list at the left and then list the opposite on the right:

Sensitive	Tough
Logical	Creative
Consistent	Unpredictable
Trusting	Cautious

  Spend some time developing the trait you are less likely to use. Say you always tackle a problem with logic; give creativity a try.

- **Retain or regain your self-confidence.** The skills for resilience begin with a focus on problems, but in the end it is the optimistic outlook that gets the best results. Some people worry that if they aren't hard on themselves they will make mistakes or set themselves up for disappointment. Both of these beliefs are self-limiting; it is positive self-efficacy that leads to success.

Further Steps

- **Develop self-efficacy**. Self-efficacy is the belief that you are capable and that your actions can have a positive effect on the outcome of an adverse situation. If you tend to believe that you are at the mercy of luck and fate, that belief will hold you back and limit your efforts because those beliefs affect the way you feel and act. If you sometimes doubt yourself and your abilities, those beliefs can be changed by examining old attitudes and then developing newer and more productive core beliefs.

- **Display your humorous side**. A good sense of humor puts people at ease, minimizes stress, and diffuses conflicts.[15] One of the lesser-known secrets of the most successful business leaders is that they get people to laugh!

- **Identify the limiting core beliefs**. Core beliefs are the most fundamental and central ideas people form about themselves. These beliefs are developed in childhood through interaction with adults as we try to gain mastery over new situations. Most of the time we have positive core beliefs, like "I can do most things competently," or "I am generally in control." Under times of crisis and distress, however, we are most susceptible to negative core beliefs. When it comes to self-efficacy, these overgeneralized, global, and absolute negative themes center around helplessness. Some of the most common are:

I am helpless.	I am inadequate.
I am weak.	I am ineffective.
I am a failure.	I am defective.
I am powerless.	I am incompetent.
I'm not good enough.	I am trapped.

- **Challenge those beliefs**. Even if you strongly feel this belief to be true, realize that this is only an idea, not necessarily the truth. The reason you maintain that belief is that you are paying attention to the supporting evidence while ignoring the evidence to the contrary. By modifying your beliefs you can begin to look for the evidence that supports a more productive and resilient core belief.

Old Belief	New Belief
I am powerless.	I have control over many things.
I am a failure.	I have had many successes.
I am defective.	I have both strengths and weaknesses.

- **Strengthen new beliefs**. What is the evidence to support the new belief? You have been filtering out all of these facts so you need to be specific and persistent.

New Belief:	I have had many successes.
Evidence to Support:	I made decisions about next year. I developed the timelines everyone uses. I understand new concepts.

Going Beyond

With a little practice you can develop specific skills that allow you to plan for life's inevitable problems, and you can even change some of the self-destructive and limiting ideas you have that might hold you back. Like Donald Trump and his Apprentices, you can find opportunities in the midst of adversity and maintain an attitude of "how to" rather than "we can't."

Resilience is one of our finer attributes and is the "ordinary magic" that sustains us through even the most traumatic of times. Elderly people who have survived spouses and even children have drawn on this trait to keep them both mentally and physically healthy and have a better quality of life. Although resilience may be largely inherited, it is something that can be learned and planned for. The resilient leader is able to consistently and persistently adapt and regain resolve. Resilient leaders convey this attitude to those around them with a sense of humor, flexibility, and an acceptance of others' shortcomings. They appreciate that those around them also may have failures but they encourage perseverance in others just as they do in themselves.

CHAPTER FIVE

Self-Control and Passion: Striving for Balance

Diamonds are nothing more than chunks of coal that stuck to their jobs.

—Malcolm Stevenson Forbes (1917–1990), publisher of *Forbes* magazine, which is today run by his son, Steve Forbes

WHILE OTHER KIDS PLAYED MARBLES or jump rope, the youngsters who later applied to *The Apprentice* were the kids who used part of their playground time to sell candy and pencils in a corner of the schoolyard. Although they wouldn't see it as a sacrifice, these kids developed an early passion for business and had the ability to stay focused on their goals. The emotional restraint that allows us to weigh short-term satisfaction against long-term achievement is exactly what it takes to reach a goal, and this group seems to have figured that out quite early in life.

When *The Apprentice* candidates were tempted with the same distractions that threaten to lead us all away from our goals, they didn't succumb to those little temptations. They seem to have been goal-directed at an early age. Their self-control has paid off, as evidenced by their success in the world of business. Self-control, however, is a little different from the other positive character traits described in this book. While there is no such thing as too much optimism, resilience, or self-awareness, an iron-clad will needs to be balanced with reason and passion. Because *The Apprentice* candidates love what they do, they make their choices out of desire rather than sacrifice.

> Because *The Apprentice* candidates love what they do, they make their choices out of desire rather than sacrifice.

Passion and Self-Control

For all of us, the struggle for self-regulation begins in earnest when we are about two to three years old. Developmentally, we are faced with a struggle between autonomy and self-doubt. In this struggle to assert our individuality, the theory goes, if we have too many restrictions, we can become rigid and obsessive, and reluctant about trying new things, but if we have too few limits, we can become overly impulsive and undisciplined. Optimally, we will develop the right degrees of both freedom of choice and self-restraint.

> While there is no such thing as too much optimism, resilience, or self-awareness, an iron-clad will needs to be balanced with reason and passion.

Self-control is one of our finer virtues as human beings, but it should be applied without an air of moral superiority that treats self-indulgence, procrastination, and wild abandon as character defects. It is a fine line to walk: too much control can lead to just as many problems as its messy counterpart. As we saw in Chapter 3, on creativity, obsessing about the future and being too concerned with organization can not only stifle creativity but also squeeze the joy and authenticity out of life. Great leaders do require strength of will, but self-control doesn't always look the same on the outside; it can take many forms, some that look more chaotic than others. Balance and flexibility are required; restraint is used in the right amount at the right time, so that spontaneity and joy aren't the sacrificial lambs. The habits of self-control begin in the toddler years, then are solidly fixed in grade-school experiences and reinforced by the approving smile of teachers. The key by-product of self-control is a feeling of mastery and self-confidence.

The notion of self-control brings forth a picture of quiet, well-mannered children patiently taking their seats in class, but there is much to be learned by those who are successful even though they don't fit that mold. While the child who is able to conform has many advantages in the classroom setting, there are very successful executives who struggled with learning difficulties in school and who overcame obstacles to achieve their hard-won success. Little Emily, who always turns her paper in on time, sits quietly with her hands folded in her lap and never seems to crease her nicely pressed outfit; she gets rewarded quite a bit for her tidy behavior. Andrew, with the chocolate ring around his mouth, the crumpled papers turned in late, and the constant urge to leap out of his seat, gets a lot less positive feedback in school, but that doesn't mean he is doomed to a life of failure. Although it is more difficult for a boisterous, distracted kid to master the kind of learning required in traditional schools, that child often

> **The key to walking the tightrope between self-control and passion is in developing restraint and self-confidence while never losing the enthusiasm for what you are doing.**

finds a way to get it in other places and goes on to excel later in life.

The full picture reveals that there are two types of highly successful people when it comes to self-control. One type has always had the ability to delay gratification and control her impulsivity as she steadfastly works her way through the maze of academic and business institutions. Although she develops self-confidence, she can later struggle maintaining passion when needed. The other type of successful person has struggled with impulse control; maybe he has even been labeled with a learning disability or an attention deficit. It isn't until he discovers what he is passionate about that he is able to reign in his impulses because he has finally found something that makes the self-sacrifice worthwhile. This latter type of executive can struggle with self-confidence because of his early experiences in school, even though he may have loads of passion for what he is doing. There are great examples of both types of leaders in both the business world and on *The Apprentice*, and their stories of success contain clues about how they made the most of their particular strengths.

> Every day we are faced with decisions big and small as an internal war is waged between the ego and id, between pleasure and restraint, between instant gratification and self-discipline.

The key to walking the tightrope between self-control and passion is in developing restraint and self-confidence while never losing the enthusiasm for what you are doing. This, then, is a tale of the people who get to the top, some of them inside the box and some of them outside.

The Marshmallow People

Abigail Adams, the wife of President John Adams, said, "Great difficulties may be surmounted by patience and perseverance." That work ethic is the very spirit that our country is founded on. It's the no-nonsense attitude of our founding fathers that still exerts a mighty influence in the public school system and in most of our institutions of work and government. Sacrifice and hard work are considered the cornerstones of business success and academic achievement.

Every day we are faced with decisions big and small as an internal war is waged between the ego and id, between pleasure and restraint, between instant gratification and self-discipline. As I sit in an apartment in New York City, the perfect Indian summer day is calling quite loudly for me to come outside and play. It is the demands of a deadline that make me ignore all the appealing sights and sounds of the city if this book is ever to be written!

As early as preschool, we face the difficult choices of giving in to temptation or showing some self-restraint. Imagine being four years old again and having an adult tell you that he is going to leave for an errand. You can have a delicious-looking marshmallow sitting there in front of you, but if you wait until the adult gets back, you can have two marshmallows.

That is just what happened in a research project conducted in the 1960s at the preschool at Stanford University.[1] The children were left alone in the room, each staring eye-to-eye with a plump, juicy marshmallow for fifteen excruciating minutes. Some of the kids fidgeted, some stared at the clock or covered their eyes, and some even sat on their hands to physically restrain themselves. Others just popped that marshmallow in their mouth the minute the researcher left the room.

> **Impulse control is one of the master aptitudes of emotional intelligence. It underscores how well people can regulate their emotions and impulses in order to pursue their long-term goals.**

Twelve to fourteen years later, when these kids were tracked down as adolescents, their management of the marshmallow incident had some amazing predictive abilities. There were dramatic differences between the children who had resisted the temptation and those who had immediately gobbled up the treat. Kids who held out for that second treat were, as teenagers, more assertive, better at handling stress, more self-reliant, confident, dependable, and trustworthy. They were more likely to take the initiative and achieve long-range goals.

Astonishingly, the marshmallow test was a better predictor of SAT scores and later college achievement than were IQ scores! Impulse control is one of the master aptitudes of emotional intelligence. It underscores how well people can regulate their emotions and impulses in order to pursue their long-term goals.

This bit of research has hopeful implications for early learning because, whereas IQ is relatively stable, the skills of emotional intelligence, such as impulse control, can be learned. Whether they learned it or were born with it, *The Apprentice* candidates have remarkable impulse-control skills. When I first met the candidates, I thought, "I have finally met the Marshmallow People."

The First Apprentice

In season one, there were three people in their early twenties who were well on their way to becoming millionaires. Consistently, the applicants for each season used planning and persistence to gain education, credentials, and business contacts to patiently feather their nests and develop their fortunes. The ultimate example of self-control and diligence from season one would have to be Bill Rancic, who ultimately won the first season.

Bill Rancic has written a book, and the picture on the cover is quite telling.[2] He looks relaxed, self-assured, pulled together, and in control. It is easy to see how this all-American, accomplished, and good-looking guy would easily fit into *The Apprentice* mold. With Bill, what you see is what you get. He is quite likable, polite, well-rounded, and normal without being boring.

In that first season, Donald Trump was excited about the prospect of a national job search with "smart, ambitious applicants." He says he had his eye on Bill from the beginning. Bill embodies many of the most salient elements of self-control. During season one, he was adaptable and applied different skills to each task, he

Bill Rancic was the winner of the first season of *The Apprentice.*

worked well with other people, and he had proved his mastery in the business world.

Indeed, hard work is Bill's mantra. He credits his pre- and post-*Apprentice* success to "hard work and dedication." He is that guy next door from the suburbs of Chicago who, at the age of ten, discovered a penchant for building businesses and making money. Bill found that if he made pancakes for his grandmother's friends, they would slip a $5 bill under the plate—and his first business concept was born. I don't know about you, but at ten years old, I was riding my bike, reading comic books, and watching Saturday morning cartoons. Not Bill. He learned from an early age that his work paid off with a remarkable feeling of mastery and accomplishment, and he was hooked. Bill would have waited for that second marshmallow.

> The skill of delaying gratification and reining in impulses is one of the main cornerstones of emotional intelligence.

The skill of delaying gratification and reining in impulses is one of the main cornerstones of emotional intelligence. It creates a fertile ground for other positive emotional traits such as adaptability and good social skills. Bill's early confidence that he could be successful gave him ease in his interactions with other people and flexibility in the way he approached problem solving. Self-confidence sets up an expectation that other people will like you; it creates a self-fulfilling prophecy because people are attracted to others who are relaxed and self-assured. That assuredness fuels the courage to try new things and the resulting success further reinforces a sense of mastery. It is another upward spiral of positive emotions that fuel positive outcomes.

Even though Bill followed the rules, worked hard, and learned from his mistakes, he didn't always fit the standard mold. His kindergarten teacher was concerned because he couldn't "stay within the lines," and his high school teachers wondered if he should switch to a trade school. His lack of interest in school didn't come from impulsiveness; it came from a vision that was beyond his peers in the classroom. When he realized that college was what would help him achieve his goals in business, he ended up graduating with honors from Loyola University.

Self-Control: Asking Questions

Bill's first job was in sales at a commodity metals firm; although he felt "above the whole thing," he realized he had a lot to learn. He observed the more seasoned salesmen, listened to the pitches that worked and those that didn't, and modeled his actions on the most successful approaches.

> Many people think it is a sign of weakness to ask questions, but asking the right questions shows flexibility, open-mindedness, and curiosity.

Bill wasn't great at traditional classroom learning, but he applied self-discipline in his efforts to expand his knowledge and experience. The principal reason he applied to *The Apprentice* was to learn everything he could from the master himself, Donald Trump. Bill remains open to learning and has self-control and patience with the sometimes tedious task of acquiring new skills.

If you didn't develop good "marshmallow skills" early in life and find yourself impatient with the process of learning, there are ways to develop your skills and make the learning process easier. Although it seems very basic, the ability to ask questions is essential in developing a learning set. Many people think it is a sign of weakness to ask questions, but asking the right questions shows flexibility, open-mindedness, and curiosity. It is also a way to develop a bond with others by showing your respect for their knowledge, your ability to collaborate on solving problems, and your genuine interest in their opinions. Like Columbo, you can get to the bottom of the matter by coming back with "one more question."

One of former Secretary of State Colin Powell's strengths is his talent to engage in dialogue to get at the truth.[3] He asks about something five different ways in order to really grasp an issue, and follows up with clarifying questions before stating his own opinion.

Remember, though, that questions should not be used to impress, dominate, embarrass, or intimidate.[4] They are most effective when used to focus on others, learn about the best way to delegate, or solidify and expand your point of view.

Self-Control: Listening to Others

Once you ask a question, the next step is to listen for the answer. High-energy, impetuous people are often mentally three steps ahead and have long ago checked out of the conversation, so they don't hear the answer. The benefit of all that great energy is the ability to multitask, getting a lot more accomplished than those who operate at a slower speed, but the drawback is the disconnection the other person feels in a conversation and the details that you sometimes miss.

> **Practicing active listening skills can both change the way you learn and improve your relationships with others.**

It sounds simplistic, but practicing active listening skills can both change the way you learn and improve your relationships with others. In our first year of graduate school, in clinical psychology, we practiced active listening. With painful awkwardness, we had to pair up and make fools of ourselves with our "let me see if I have this right" rephrasing of what we had just heard. I have to admit, however, that it has become second nature for me to do this, confirming what I have just heard, and I believe I have learned more this way by really listening when others speak.

The added benefit of active listening is that it is quite a valuable commodity in a business setting. Many people do not really listen; if you are one of the few who pay attention, by default you will be privy to information that others will miss, and as the old saying goes, "knowledge is power."

> Many people do not really listen; if you are one of the few who pay attention, by default you will be privy to information that others will miss.

You have probably practiced active listening in at least of few of your business seminars, so you may want just to dust off your notes and put some of the ideas into practice. I know it seems forced at first, but with time you will develop a natural way of paying attention to others that is warm and sincere and will be genuinely appreciated. Some of the basics of good listening are listed in "The Guide for Self-Control" at the end of this chapter under "Initial Steps."

Building Self-Confidence

Although our confidence in our own abilities is shaped by many different factors, we have received much feedback from how well we have performed in school. The children who develop verbal skills early in life (and girls have an advantage in this arena), and who are less impulsive and less likely to blurt out answers to questions, are primed to do well in school. All of those gold stars and approving smiles from the teacher go a long way to foster self-confidence.

But self-confidence can be developed in other arenas as well, as was the case with Bill Rancic. Bill didn't flourish in school until he got to college, but he was quite self-confident in other ways. Bill's father helped build his self-confidence as a child. He told Bill to never be afraid of failure and to stand up tall and try his best, but that if he didn't succeed that was OK, too. That approach sends the all-important message that failures are not to be taken personally and that the crucial thing is to try.

Although he didn't make it as far as Bill Rancic, Raj Bhakta, from season two, was unshakably self-confident. Raj is a tad more impulsive than Bill in some arenas, but every bit as charming and self-confident. Raj was twenty-eight at the time he was on the show, and he had earned degrees in both economics and history. His business successes are impressive: he founded Automovia Technology Partners when he was only twenty-three, and then created Vanquish Enterprises, a venture in the real estate sector involving hotel, retail, and condominium projects in the upscale ski resort of Vail, Colorado. He could have been selected to do

Raj Bhakta, from season two, was unshakably self-confident.

the show on pure merit, but his eccentricity and charm helped to seal the deal.

His bow ties and the occasional walking cane are his trademarks: he has been wearing the bow ties since eleventh grade. Besides adhering to traditional, old-fashioned values, Raj claims the ties show respect for his idol, Winston Churchill. His self-confidence has been labeled an "oversized ego," which could explain Raj's fascination with Napoleon Bonaparte and his ability to recite Napoleon's speeches. Even during just the first episode, he referred to Caesar's empire building, Joseph Stalin's platform shoes, and several British battleships.[5] If you have never seen Raj and he is beginning to sound pretentious and pompous, let me reassure you that his approach is tempered with ample charm and intelligence.

Although Raj is in the real estate business, he was fired on the show as project manager on a task to renovate a house in New Jersey. He made quite a few mistakes, but the next day he appeared on the *Today* show and didn't show any signs of self-doubt. When Katie Couric asked him his plans for the future, he replied that, while he certainly could pursue his "billion dollar" business prospects, he had decided to enter the political arena. Katie asked where he got his healthy dose of self-confidence, and he replied, "From my Jewish grandmother."

> What Bill and Raj have in common is the ability to weather the effects of mistakes without letting them impact their self-assessment.

Raj was referring to a Jewish woman who lived nearby when he was growing up. He visited her quite often, and she adored him and told him he was destined to do great things, and would one day grow up to be "the governor." Raj's father came from India, and being the only son gave Raj a special stature in a family with four older sisters. His Irish mother contributed a feisty temper and enough reality checks to keep him from getting egomaniacal. The eclectic heritage worked, and Raj is a delightful example of healthy self-confidence.

What Bill and Raj have in common is the ability to weather the effects of mistakes without letting them impact their self-assessment. It is the opposite of impulsive "emotional hijacking," which would leave them feeling anxious and depressed. In fact, Raj's firing could be viewed as an instructional guide on building self-confidence.

Raising Your Self-Esteem

Raj and Bill both gained self-respect and self-control from the adults in their lives. Likewise, our ideas of self-worth come largely from our interactions and relationships with the important care-givers in our life. Raj heard the message that he was destined for greatness, while Bill heard that he was loved and appreciated even if he made a mistake.

Not everyone is so lucky. More impulsive, creative, and spontaneous individuals often receive invalid negative messages about their self-worth. For those who found it hard to conform to the many spoken and unspoken rules of early school years, their experiences were more likely full of disapprovals. Some very successful executives have mentioned painful experiences they had in school that left them with a fear of "being found out." But even those of us who have developed unproductive beliefs about our self-worth should know that those beliefs can be changed.

> Some very successful executives have mentioned painful experiences they had in school that left them with a fear of "being found out."

The core beliefs you have about your worth can affect your thoughts, actions, and most importantly, your overall mood and how you feel in given situations. The sequence begins with a belief and ends with a feeling. To illustrate, imagine that you are placed in charge of a short-term work group. You have to come up with a recruiting advertising campaign for the NYPD in forty-eight hours. You are told by the agency that the ad campaign should, above all, appeal to the heart. Your team consists of ener-

getic, opinionated, Type As who bristle at being led. There is tremendous infighting because everyone is certain he or she has a
better idea than you, the leader. You stand by your convictions,
fight the team, and don't take the attacks to heart. Your team ends
up winning. The other team leader has a moment of uncharacter-
istic self-doubt, wavers, has negative feelings, and ends up adopting an idea she doesn't really believe in. Her team loses.

Group dynamics, product, and materials are all the same. The
independent variable in this situation is the underlying self-
confidence of the leader that serves as a lens to "focus" the intentions of the team. If this sounds familiar, it is because it happened
during season two, and it illustrates the huge effect that self-
confidence can have on leadership.

Once you are aware of the relationship between your beliefs
about your ability and the effect they can have on your leadership
and decision-making ability, you can begin to make adjustments.
Most of us have some areas of supreme self-confidence and other
areas where we feel we could use improvement. Self-confidence
can also waiver in moments of extreme stress.

If you think that some self-defeating beliefs are affecting your
self-confidence, see the final section of this chapter, "The Guide
for Self-Control and Passion," for suggestions on modifying unhelpful attitudes. Like Raj, you can become impervious to that
sinking feeling and unproductive self-doubt—and you won't even
have to wear a bow tie.

The Exceptions to the Rule

Most contestants on seasons one and two of *The Apprentice*
nicely fit the mold of self-control. The cast consisted mostly of
solid citizens who had climbed the academic and corporate lad-
ders to earn impressive degrees and achieve financial success.
Graduates of law schools, business schools, and the Ivy League
colleges all lined up as models of decorum and self-restraint.
Even the street-smart contestants who hadn't taken the academic

route had nonetheless attended real estate schools or had created businesses of their own since high school.

Then, season three came along with a different type of contestant. Every season of every reality show has a theme that emerges during the casting process. Religion, family background, physical appearance, even musical ability seem to cluster in certain seasons. For some reason, the theme of season three was impatience with traditional learning, even among many of the contestants who had attended college.

Most applicants found school to be extremely confining. Regardless of their IQs, they complained that they were easily bored in class, had difficulty staying in their seats, and couldn't wait to get out of school every day. Some of them got in trouble for talking too much or being the class clown; some just struggled quietly to make it through what they saw as a complete waste of time. The bigger plans of business deals and money-making ventures had to be put on hold until they were old enough to put them into practice.

> At its inception, *The Apprentice* was conceived as a test of whether someone with street smarts or someone with an Ivy League education would more likely have what it takes to rise to the top in the Trump Corporation.

The minute these people were free of the rules and restrictions of school, they blossomed. Great opportunities were waiting for them, and finally free, they exploded onto the business scene, ready to make their marks. Most of them didn't fit the pedigreed and polished mold of season two applicants, but their stories were heartwarming and endearing, and their successes quite impressive.

Street Smarts vs. Book Learning

At its inception, *The Apprentice* was conceived as a test of whether someone with street smarts or someone with an Ivy League education would more likely have what it takes to rise to the top in the Trump Corporation. Given the season three contestant pool, it was clearly primed to test that hypothesis. In previous seasons the teams had been divided into men and women, but in season three the divisions were along education lines. Team Magna was composed of people with degrees ranging from bachelor's to doctor of jurisprudence. Team Net Worth consisted of street-savvy folks who had bypassed academia and set about making money; they chose their name based on the fact that, as a group, their net worth far exceeded that of the book-smart crowd.

Many of the street-smart group had struggled with traditional education, and a few people in the book-smart team had the same experience. Although most of them had never actually been given an official diagnosis of attention deficit disorder (ADD), some had suspected as much. We know that impulse control is central to later success in life and in business, so how can the remarkable achievements of these candidates be explained?

The powerful executives who have spoken out about their struggles with learning disabilities like dyslexia or ADD include Charles Schwab, the chairman of the discount brokerage firm; John Chambers, chief executive of Cisco Systems; Richard Branson, founder of the Virgin Group; Barbara Corcoran, founder of the Corcoran Group real estate firm; David Neeleman, chief executive of JetBlue Airways; and the late computer pioneer William Hewlett. They have voiced the sentiment that, although they struggled with learning problems in school, they gained important managerial skills as they adapted and grew into their own person.

> We know that impulse control is central to later success in life and in business, so how can the remarkable achievements of these candidates be explained?

At sixty-six, Charles Schwab is able to think back to the moments in school when he knew something was wrong but was afraid to talk about it.[6] He says that it wasn't until his son was diagnosed with dyslexia about fifteen years ago that he even had a name for what he experienced. He had always been good at math and athletics, but when it came to English he had a "nasty secret." To this day, he is a painfully slow reader, and he credits his golf game for getting him into Stanford University. What he realizes now is that, even though he didn't excel in school, he had other talents and skills that have given him an advantage in the business world. Like many executives with dyslexia, Charles Schwab is able to see things in a nonconventional way and has been many steps ahead of his contemporaries.

> **Like many executives with dyslexia, Charles Schwab is able to see things in a nonconventional way and has been many steps ahead of his contemporaries.**

A distinguishing feature of people with learning disabilities is that, in order to survive the traditional school system, they have become adept at thinking outside the box. In the process, they develop resilience, adaptability, and creativity. It is estimated that one-fifth of the population has some form of learning disability, but among overachievers and top business executives, the proportion is much higher.[7] Their novel way of looking at things is a handicap in the traditional classroom setting, but is an asset in business, especially as entrepreneurs.

Beneficial "Deficits"

The benefits of these "disabilities" include intuitiveness, creativity, high energy, and enthusiasm. Calling the conditions disorders is unfortunate because there are both problems and advantages to each. A component of ADD is a tendency to daydream. Students with ADD are usually quite bright, have trouble attending and staying put, impulsively say what comes to mind, and find distractions difficult to resist. You can't help but be impressed by the list of people with ADD who have unique talents and undeniable gifts. Thomas Edison was at the bottom of his class, Albert Einstein was expelled, and John Irving nearly flunked out of school.

It was not until 1980 that the term *attention deficit disorder*, with or without hyperactivity, was coined.[8] Its first mention as a clinical description was in 1902, when it was labeled *morbid defect of moral control*. In the mid-1700s, when Mozart lived, his parents and contemporaries only knew that he was restless, impulsive, impatient, distractible, energetic, and innovative. Historians note how hyperactive and distractible he was, and his reported eccentricities and frenetic energy closely resemble the behaviors we now call attention deficit hyperactivity disorder (ADHD).[9] Although his contemporaries found his music too difficult to understand, Mozart has given the world some of the most complex, intricate, and beautiful music ever written. Ahead of his time and brilliant enough to remain one of the most influential composers in history, Mozart exemplifies the gifts of impulsivity and distractible energy.

> Ahead of his time and brilliant enough to remain one of the most influential composers in history, Mozart exemplifies the gifts of impulsivity and distractible energy.

Season three had its own impulsive, distractible, and extremely creative music composer on Team Magna. Danny Kastner is not only an exceptionally talented musician and composer, but he is also the creator and owner of a company called POPstick, which designs striking Web-based interactive technology to market new products for Fortune 500 companies. He looks a bit like Austin Powers, "Man of Mystery," with his 1970s shag haircut and an assortment of bright rainbow-colored polyester suits. He is uncontrollable, full of enthusiasm, and absolutely certain that everyone loves him.

Grade school was Danny's playground, and he remembers that he was the "ADD kid," kind of "wacky and running around." It was before the official ADD diagnosis had been coined, and he wasn't given medication, but once he reached adulthood he got a clear-cut diagnosis. He was a handful to his teachers, but most fell under the spell of his charms.

Relatively bored by books and tradition, Danny nonetheless

Danny Kastner, from season three, has a talent for making passion and impulsivity work to his advantage.

got straight As with the right kind of teacher. On the other hand, his trigonometry grades suffered because he didn't like the teacher and was bored with the class. After early graduation at age 17, he went straight to Cleveland State University, although he wasn't the "collegiate" type and was there only to study music. A big fish in a little pond, he hired eighty performers for his senior recital, including a choir and an orchestra, and he wrote all the music in his typical over-the-top style.

School was no longer boring and he went on to graduate school at Boston University. He still had a love-hate relationship with the classroom but worked hard to get ahead whenever he was recognized and challenged. For one class, a paper was required to meet the course requirement, but Danny didn't see it as relevant; he wrote the paper but was so fed up with the academic nature of the program that didn't encourage creative expression that he never handed it in. Not one to leave that marshmallow for later, he never bothered to apply for the "piece of paper" degree, even though he had all the required credits. Danny believes that it was the mass that he wrote that won two national awards that was the true testimony of his graduate school achievement.

In that last year of graduate school Danny founded a company called Scores International, which created software to print sheet music. His love of computers nearly matched his love of music, and in graduate school and business he found a way to marry his two interests and founded POPstick. Microsoft, Xerox, and Accenture were among the first companies that subscribed to his service. The company is thriving under his creative and fun-loving management style.

> You have to wonder what would have become of Mozart if he had an Apple computer.

Creative ideas seem to bubble up out of Danny almost nonstop, and the ideas are good. He is at the opposite end of the "marshmallow continuum," but his talent and passion make impulsivity work to his advantage. Business school and marketing and accounting classes may have eluded him, yet he has the vision and enthusiasm that is vital in today's technology-focused business world. You have to wonder what would have become of Mozart if he had an Apple computer!

When you contrast someone like Danny with someone like Bill Rancic from season one, you see the two different approaches to self-control. Bill is neatly self-controlled and fueled by hard work and persistence; Danny is chaotic and messy and fueled by passion and energy. Danny can lock himself in his room for days to compose and not be distracted. Bill Rancic can shoulder hard work as well, but in a more planned and organized way.

The two of them even look their parts. Danny, with his messy shoulder-length shag, glasses slightly askew, is in sharp contrast to Bill's chiseled looks, short hair, and crisp designer suits. But both Danny and Bill have capitalized on their unique talents to make impressive dents in the business world at a relatively young age. What Danny lacked in impulse control he more than made up for in enthusiasm and passion.

Passion: The Flip Side of Self-Control

It is interesting that a "disorder of attention" as described in the previous section can also be accompanied by passionate and energetic interests. That distractibility has also been called a heightened awareness; to have passion means to be deeply affected and emotionally moved by outside influences. Being passionate in your work carries over into all other aspects of life and requires letting yourself be stirred by the events of the day, both big and small.

> Being passionate in your work carries over into all other aspects of life and requires letting yourself be stirred by the events of the day, both big and small.

Many an experienced and seasoned executive has found, after years of good impulse control, that he inexplicably has trouble getting motivated and fired up about what he is doing. Recognizing this, business leaders have written about the importance of having a "passion for excellence" and a "fire in the belly." One of the most exciting things about working with people in their twenties is their sense of wonder and their zest for everything that is new to them. Their enthusiasm can infuse seasoned, jaded executives with a renewed sense of accomplishment. Indeed, passion is contagious; energetic people inject others with energy. In the European sense of having an apprentice, older, seasoned experts take younger, enthusiastic students under their wings in what is a mutually rewarding relationship. Experience and passion blend nicely to yield successful results.

But caution: passion can easily fade if taken for granted. The act of balancing self-control and passion is not easy; joy and passion are easily lost along the way in an effort to exercise discipline and strength of will. We've already discussed ways to increase self-control; passion can wax and wane over a career, but there are some things you can do to foster more zest and joy when it doesn't come easily.

Finding Your Passion

Coach Vince Lombardi said, "If you aren't fired with enthusiasm, you will be fired with enthusiasm." During a season one task to sell artwork, the losing team picked an artist they weren't crazy about, but they chose her because her work had a high selling price. In the postanalysis of what went wrong, Donald Trump made the point that you have to believe in what you are selling. People quickly sniff out insincerity, making it tremendously challenging to lead if the project is something you have no passion for.

If you aren't passionate about what you do, do some deep, dark, soul-searching and use some brutal honesty to find out what is missing from your work. There are different stages of a career during which different motivations are the driving force. In Abraham Maslow's hierarchy of needs, the pyramid has basic food, shelter, and safety at the base; social and self-esteem needs in the center; and what he called self-actualization at the tip of the pyramid. Passion is the force at this tip. It makes sense that those at the executive level are more likely to struggle with this need, as they have already worked their way up the pyramid.

> If you aren't passionate about what you do, do some deep, dark, soul-searching and use some brutal honesty to find out what is missing from your work.

Early in life you can get tremendously excited about any job that pays money. I was thrilled about one of my first jobs silk-screening tee-shirts because it was just so alluring to have a job and to make money. Later in my career I was motivated by social and self-esteem needs, and I was full of anticipation and excitement on Sunday night about getting back to work at a large, well-known law firm with lots of smart and interesting people. I was only an assistant librarian, but I shelved books and delivered mail as if it were the most important job in the firm.

At the executive level, it is unlikely that the passion is about money or even self-esteem. At that level, it likely revolves around becoming self-actualized and finding the job you were meant to do if you haven't already found it. As the workforce changes, more and more people are reaching this level of the pyramid at much earlier points in their careers. Because these employees expect to be well paid, they now also believe they are entitled to jobs that are fun, that are cool, that let them discover who they really are. Increasingly, work is not just a way to get a paycheck; it is also a way to be self-fulfilled. Richard Barton, the thirty-year-old in charge of Microsoft Expedia, echoed the sentiments of psychologist Abraham Maslow when he said that, "Work is not work. It's a hobby you happen to get paid for."[10]

Abraham Maslow, who greatly influenced the world of organizational and industrial psychology, is still a vital voice in the twenty-first century. Many executives hit a wall when they are no longer emotionally involved in their work. This is typically due to their not working at something they truly love or they don't consider to be truly important. Self-actualization, as defined by Maslow, is an intricate concept that blends several of our highest aspirations. It involves striving to fulfill your destiny—to become what has always burned inside you. Another aspect is to be committed to important and worthwhile work that you identify with and consider truly important.

Truly happy people work well at something they consider genuinely important. It is the difference between trudging through days at work and being excited on Sunday night about returning to work on Monday. Maslow likened finding one's calling to the embrace of two people who belong together—that by listening to your own "impulse voice" and acting on free will, you embrace your fate as eagerly as you would pick your ideal mate.

> Author and poet Samuel Ullman wrote, "Years may wrinkle the skin, but to give up enthusiasm wrinkles the soul."

True, there are bills to be paid and people you don't want to let down. Just because you aren't at the very base of the pyramid doesn't mean you can quit your day job and try out for the National League at the age of fifty. There could be a price to pay. Too much soul searching could lead to making irresponsible changes in a career that pays the bills and is safe and comfortable. There is also a high price to pay when you deny your unique destiny. Author and poet Samuel Ullman wrote, "Years may wrinkle the skin, but to give up enthusiasm wrinkles the soul." But when you aren't embracing your own true nature at work, it is like being in a bad marriage—like an artist trying to be an accountant or an accountant trying to be an artist.

There is no simple "how to" when it comes to finding what your soul wants. It can be an uncomfortable process of sleepless nights, glaring honesty, and moments of anxiety and depression, as you threaten to shake up a dull but safe and secure way of life. A lot of fears and worries can surface, but the good thing about a crisis is that, even under unsettling circumstances, it produces needed change.

My family has a story about me and my brother when I was ten and he was five. He was having a very bad day, so I put my arm around him and took him to the other room. We sat and talked for some time, and when we came back he was happy and smiling. My Mom asked what I had said, and I replied that it just took "a little psychology." Later, in ninth grade, when we learned to write our first term paper, I gravitated to a small red book in our library called *The Ego and the Id* by Sigmund Freud.

In college I seemed to rack up enough credits for a psychology major without even thinking about it. Sadly, I was still at the bottom of the needs hierarchy when I graduated with a B.A. in psychology. I was a single parent with a young daughter to care for. My adviser warned me that graduate school would take about six years, followed by supervised work and a dissertation, all for little or no money. Talk about delaying gratification! I joined the Air Force instead and got the immediate gratification of money and travel.

For no apparent reason, after I left the Air Force and took a job as the office manager in the University of California, Riverside, Computer Science Department, I began to cry all the time. I was quite organized, efficient, and good at managing the office, but on Monday mornings I was filled with a black dread. During some honest and open conversations with Susan Hawkins, a good friend and student who worked in our department, I realized I still longed to be a psychologist, and with my daughter ready to graduate, the time was finally right. I registered for the Graduate Record Examination (qualifying exam for graduate school) that same afternoon.

I stopped crying that day, and I also stopped having a recurrent dream I'd had for years about being back at my old locker in high school. My destiny was trying to tell me that I wasn't finished yet. Through battles with dissertation professors and weighty student loans there were moments of frustration, but never any doubt or uncertainty. Finally, I have recaptured that Sunday night feeling of eager anticipation about getting back to work.

> When you get that dried and withered feeling about what you are doing, it is an undeniable message that something isn't singing your name.

When you get that dried and withered feeling about what you are doing, it is an undeniable message that something isn't singing your name. Maybe it doesn't require a huge career change; maybe it is just time to start a new project or make changes in the day. Or maybe it requires a change from within.

Not a Simple Task

Thousands of dollars are spent every day by large corporations offering business seminars to spark and stoke the fires that motivate people in their jobs. The problem is that human nature is complex and can't always be neatly boxed into the Myers-Briggs Type Indicator codes of, for example, "ISFJ" or "ENTP" (codes that designate whether a person is introverted or extroverted; sensing or intuitive; feeling or thinking; and organized or spontaneous). Workshops designed to reignite passion at work fail to adequately acknowledge our diversity and the need we have to self-actualize.

We have come to expect our lessons to come in smaller and smaller sound bites. They come packaged for us to learn in one afternoon, often as ten easy steps to management or five types of difficult people you will encounter at work. Self-help has served a good purpose, but it was never meant to imply that honesty, passion, and self-actualization would come easily or could be reduced to a few simple steps. The reward for the difficult work is being energized, interested, and well suited to the task. It may take soul-searching to get to the top of the pyramid, but you will be rewarded with a great view.

> It may take soul-searching to get to the top of the pyramid, but you will be rewarded with a great view.

Self-Control, Risk, and the Entrepreneur

When it comes right down to it, the characteristic shared by Olympic athletes, world-class artists and musicians, and high-level executives and entrepreneurs is the motivation to push themselves in relentless pursuit of their passions. Often, they win out by simply putting in more hours than the other guy, whether it is fueled by diligence or ardent enthusiasm.

During a task postmortem in season three, it came out that one of the losing teams' members had taken a nap, and George indignantly asked why the individual would sleep when there was a competition going on. His point was that they were young and presumably hungry for a win; sleep could come later. Although it may seem a bit extreme, his position is that, at that level of competition, effort should be fierce and unrelenting. If you want something badly enough, you have that steely resolve to resist the single marshmallow and stay focused on the bigger prize.

Their ultimate boss, Donald Trump, after all, is a self-proclaimed workhorse.[11] He has said that if he had maintained his normal work ethic in the 1970s and part of the 1980s, he wouldn't have had a fall into bankruptcy. Before this tough lesson, he was lulled into complacency by his success, he didn't stay focused, and he let himself relax and take it easy. Now he is back on top and in full swing keeping to his normal disciplined schedule. A typical day for him is fast-paced and packed with appointments.

Up by 5:30 A.M. every morning, Trump reads the daily papers and drinks a Diet Coke.[12] By 9:00 A.M., he begins a morning of hourly meetings. Real estate, publishing, television, beauty pageants—it all piques his interest. He rarely stops for lunch, preferring to grab something between projects, and then he is back for a full afternoon of telephone calls and conferences. By 6:00 P.M. or so he heads back to his apartment in Trump Tower, but his workday never really ends—he prefers it that way. The idea of a vacation doesn't appeal to him, and when he does take a holiday he brings along plenty of work.

Elbow grease aside, there are two distinctive entrepreneurial qualities that Trump and many of *The Apprentice* candidates possess, and those are a willingness to take risks and a fondness for creating new enterprises. During a boardroom in season three, the differences between the diligent executive and the entrepreneur were distilled to the simplest of terms.

It was the night that Bren Olswanger, a district attorney from Memphis, was fired. Bren admitted that he had been averse to taking risks most of his life, and he acknowledged that the riskiest thing he had ever done was quit his job as a D.A. to compete on *The Apprentice*. Donald Trump answered that while he wasn't a "big fan" of taking risks, it was something that is required of the entrepreneur.

Although Bren said he was willing to learn, Donald wondered if risk-taking wasn't more an inborn trait. Donald stood by his belief that his final Apprentice should have a talent for developing businesses and a willingness to take risks. The fierce drive that Donald spoke of is the quality that makes the show so compelling, as the candidates compete with such intensity.

Yes, their risk-taking and enthusiasm about creating businesses make it all look like fun. Although Bren was averse to risks, he had that same passion for business that is common to the candidates. It was quite a surprise for me to learn that these business-minded people are so vibrant and interesting. The gold standard in my family has always been education. No one ever talked about or appeared that interested in making money.

My earliest impression of businessmen was from the movie *Mary Poppins*. The children's father, Mr. Banks, spent long, dry days at the adding machine in the vault of the bank and would come home stern and grumpy. He didn't play with the children; he rarely smiled or laughed; he didn't even want to fly a kite!

> An entrepreneurial spirit isn't just about the cold process of making money; it is about taking chances and carrying through on your ideas for doing new things.

During the first season of *The Apprentice*, I slowly began to change my mind. How excited the contestants became at the prospect of a new venture! I realized that an entrepreneurial spirit isn't just about the cold process of making money; it is about taking chances and carrying through on your ideas for doing new things. Some of us are interested in learning theories and abstraction, but the entrepreneur is interested in seeing the fruits of his labors—labors with a practical, tangible focus.

Entrepreneurs could never be satisfied sticking to the practice of law; they would have to own the firm or use their legal knowledge in new ways. When I think of all of the promising and talented entrepreneurs who have applied to the show, the person at the top of that list would be Brian McDowell, from season three.

With an Irish twinkle in his eye and a temper to match, Brian stands about 5 feet 2 inches, is stocky, and has a voice that is always turned up a notch or two. True to his speculative nature, he knew his final task would be a make-or-break situation. Loyalty is just part of his makeup, and he was reluctant to drag his team members through the mud. His first instinct was to take full responsibility for losing the competition, and Donald Trump eventually let him take the bullet. But if Trump had gotten to know

Brian, he would have found that they share a love of crafting new enterprises.

Brian is that entrepreneur Trump spoke of when he asked if risk-taking wasn't an inborn trait.

When he was five years old, every Thursday morning Brian would wait for the trash truck because he knew he could make $2.50 helping the garbage collectors roll the trash cans down the driveways. When he was nine years old, his mom found a time-card machine, and he actually punched in and punched out when he did jobs on his to-do list. If he worked extra, he got overtime.

In fifth grade, Brian began buying bulk candy, gum, baseball cards, and mechanical pencils in bulk. He fashioned a makeshift store out of a box, and at recess he set up The School Store. At first it was fine, but when the kids began playing with their loot during classes he was found out and eventually was suspended. While he was away on suspension, the school opened up its own store and Brian got his first lesson in the ways of corporate America.

> That year at summer camp, Brian took one look around and realized it was a world of opportunity; his fellow campmates were locked up and away from any competition for thirty days.

That year at summer camp, Brian took one look around and realized it was a world of opportunity; his fellow campmates were locked up and away from any competition for thirty days. He was ten years old and a much younger version of "Red" from the film *The Shawshank Redemption*. He was the one who could figure out how to get anything. For the next three summers, he had his mom supply him with candy, packets of ice tea, comic books—whatever the kids wanted.

When he was nine years old, he started his first real business, Kidco. For Christmas that year he asked for a lawnmower, a weed-whacker, and a snow shovel. He charged $3 to cut a small lawn; he soon had a solid customer base, making as much as $100 each week. When he moved to a different neighborhood with larger lawns, he bought a power mower, added new clients, and kept the customers in his old neighborhood; he was making $250 each week by the age of eleven.

When Brian was thirteen, he stumbled onto a magic show and was fascinated. He found a tuxedo and a hat at a second-hand store, bought some props, and learned a few tricks. He put on his first show for $10, and he still has that $10 bill framed. By the age of fifteen, he was performing every weekend at libraries, kids' shows, law firms, schools, and corporations, and he was making $125 a show. He quickly realized that when someone asked if he also had balloons or clowns, he could rent them and make a profit. It wasn't long before Brian the Magnificent was a full-fledged entertainment business and Kidco became McDowell Landscaping. Brian split his school weeks between traditional classes and trade school, and ended up with a full scholarship to Williamson Trade College to study carpentry and business. He started in July after high school ended and lasted three months, but left because he longed to get back to business.

> He found a tuxedo and a hat at a second-hand store, bought some props, and learned a few tricks. He put on his first show for $10, and he still has that $10 bill framed.

His girlfriend from Michigan was to visit for Fourth of July weekend; he went to sleep one night wondering what they could do when she got to Philadelphia. He dreamed that he was at the park selling glow necklaces (plastic tubes of glowing material that people wear around their necks in the dark at concerts and festivals). He bought a carton of necklaces the next day, sold them immediately, and made some money; by the Fourth of July, Brian was buying glow necklaces by the case. It wasn't long before he signed a five-year lease with the owner of a local pier to sell glow necklaces at a concession stand. He was the third highest grossing vendor on the pier, and that was when he was working only three hours each night.

Brian has now turned that entrepreneurial talent toward the real estate market, but he is always seeking his next venture in any field. When he looks at something, he sees a faster, smarter, more lucrative way of doing that same thing; it is just his nature. He falls at both ends of the self-control continuum: highly inventive, passionate, and impulsive, he is at the same time disciplined and self-controlled enough to have worked ten- to fourteen-hour days since grade school.

While self-control is key to achieving excellence, the motivation to seek that excellence can come from a love of learning or from a passion for innovation. Impulse control plays a large role in school and in business, but it is especially important in those early school years when the mastery of learning builds self-esteem. Impulsive, creative, and naturally talented entrepreneurs may have to wait a little longer to have their talents recognized, but their drive to succeed gets them through. They eventually embrace self-control, fueled by their passion for what they do.

> Impulsive, creative, and naturally talented entrepreneurs may have to wait a little longer to have their talents recognized, but their drive to succeed gets them through.

For most of us who fall between the gifted entrepreneur and the gifted student, we must balance self-control with passion, knowing which to use at the right time. The following section elaborates on the suggestions made earlier in this chapter for developing those skills.

The Guide for Self-Control and Passion

Initial Steps

At the heart of self-control is a willingness to learn from new experiences and new situations. The simple skills of asking questions and then carefully listening to the answers can help you learn from any new situation.

- **Ask questions**. Questions aren't just a superficial way of warming someone up. They also aren't intended to impress. Asked with sincerity, questions go a long way toward developing relationships and allowing you to expand your knowledge. Realizing that you don't know everything isn't a weakness—it is a sign that you are capable of solving problems and that you are unlikely to bulldoze your way to a solution. Although questions can persuade, delegate, or show interest, the questions that facilitate learning are to verify or confirm information.

- **Mentally rehearse to combat assumptions**. During the final task in season three, Olympic athletes were on hand to help out with a charity event. One of the final two contestants had arranged for caterers to provide lunch and snacks for the athletes as well as their agents. Donald Trump had spoken to the athletes at one point in the event, and they complained that they hadn't gotten any food. When he asked the project manager if she had asked the athletes about the food or had made sure they had enough to eat, she said that she had *assumed* they would have let her know if there were a problem. You could see people wince as the "a" word came out of her mouth. Asking questions saves you from all of the things you *know* and *presume* to be facts. Once again, mental rehearsal before a big event can be a lifesaver. It will help you anticipate some bumps in the road and ease you into the questioning mindset.

- **Use active listening**. Listening skills help you process the information you get from asking questions. As the Bible says, "Be swift to hear and slow to speak." The following attending skills will help you actively listen:

    Open your posture.

    Lean toward the speaker.

    Maintain eye contact.

    Relax while attending.

It takes practice, but after time this questioning habit can become second nature. An open posture (arms uncrossed and relaxed shoulders) and leaning in toward the speaker help to communicate a willingness to listen. Maintaining eye contact also communicates interest, and relaxing helps you settle in to really listen instead of nervously focusing on what you will say next.

- **Paraphrase the answers**. Paraphrasing involves restating a message in a slightly different manner help to test your understanding of what was said and to communicate that you are understanding what is being said. You are trying to get at the root of what the person is both saying and feeling. If you are successful, it means that you have followed what the person was saying. For example:

  > SPEAKER: I never know what to expect from my boss because he asks for one thing and wants another.

  > LISTENER: He really confuses you.

  > SPEAKER: Yes, I get so upset because he never tells me what he really wants and then I look incompetent.

  > LISTENER: You aren't getting a clear expectation and it's frustrating.

- **Clarify, check, and summarize**. With the steps above you are well on your way to being a much better listener. Here are just a few things to tie up loose ends. When the conversation is vague or confusing, you can clarify by asking, "We have jumped around a little and I'm wondering if I have it right. Did you mean . . . ?" After you paraphrase, you can also occasionally check in by asking, "Did I get that right?" At the end of the conversation, you can summarize by stating, "We have talked about a lot today, but your main points seem to be . . ." Try these skills and you will see that you are you taking a learning approach, becoming more informed, and are less likely to jump to erroneous conclusions. The pleasant side effect is that people will feel more drawn to you because of the interest you have shown in what they have to say.

Further Steps

- **Improve self-confidence**. Self-confidence is the positive belief that you are lovable and that you "measure up" to the task at hand. If you were that unconventional type of student who didn't quite fit the mold in school, you can tend to believe, after all those years of struggling, that you aren't quite good enough. In general, boys can get negative messages about measuring up in grade school as they are usually very physically active and develop verbal skills a little more slowly than do girls. Later, in high school, girls' self-esteem can suffer, as they tend to develop math and science skills more slowly than do the boys. This is a generalization and it doesn't account for individuals, but as a whole school can impact self-esteem in this and other ways. Cognitive therapy, a practical and easy-to-understand branch of psychology, involves examining thoughts and core beliefs that result from these formative experiences and looking at the impact of those beliefs. If those beliefs are holding you back, they can be changed and replaced with more productive core beliefs.

- **Identify core beliefs about yourself**. In Chapter 4, we talked about core beliefs and self-efficacy. Core beliefs are the most fundamental and central judgments that people form about themselves in early childhood. Negative core beliefs that affect self-confidence can surface during stressful times and can impact not only how you feel but also your behavior. Over time these beliefs can be reinforced by the resulting consequences. For example, if in a certain situation you feel inadequate for the job, you are less likely to take action. Because you didn't get a chance to prove yourself, you feel even more inadequate.

When it comes to self-worth, these overgeneralized, global, and absolute negative themes center on being unlovable. Some of the most common are:

I am unlovable.	I am undesirable.
I am defective.	I am unattractive.
I am different.	I am bound to be rejected.
I am uncared for.	I am bound to be alone.

- **Challenge those beliefs**. Even if you strongly feel this belief to be true, realize that this is only an idea, not necessarily the truth. Core beliefs are rooted in childhood incidents that were probably not true at the time and are certainly no longer applicable. The belief is maintained by paying attention to evidence that supports the belief but ignoring evidence to the contrary. By transforming those beliefs you can begin to look for the evidence that supports a more productive and resilient core belief.

Old Belief	New Belief
I am unlovable.	I'm generally a likeable person.
I am unattractive.	I have many attractive qualities.
I am undesirable.	I am normal, with strengths and weaknesses.

- **Strengthen new beliefs**. What is the evidence to support the new belief? You have been filtering out all these facts, so you need to be specific and persistent.

New Belief:	I am not bound to be rejected.
Evidence to Support:	I had a proposal accepted last year.

I have good friends who value
my ideas.

Last week everyone listened to
my ideas in our meeting.

Going Beyond

Whether you are hyper, high-energy, and easily excitable, or slow,
steadfast, and determined, the decision to strive for more than
mediocrity involves a commitment to a goal.

Some of the lawyers and the MBAs on *The Apprentice* have
had a tough time being creative, but that isn't always the case.
Some of the entrepreneurs have had difficulties with planning and
discipline, but that too is variable. What most of them have
learned is to how to develop new skills and to be proud of their
strengths. They realize that they have gravitated toward what they
are best in and that they can work to add skills they are lacking.
Their common ground is the intensity and passion they have for
what they do and the self-control they have developed over the
years to achieve any goal they desire, including making it on *The
Apprentice*.

During season three, when Donald Trump was saying goodbye to six of the candidates who had come back to help in the
final task, Danny Kastner, the musician of the bunch, pulled out
his guitar to sing a song about his experience to Carolyn, George,
and Donald. It was the first time anyone had broken into song in
the boardroom! There is no doubt that Danny has a natural gift
for composing, and Trump told him that perhaps he made a better
musician than a leader. He encouraged Danny to follow his
dreams. Trump's final words as they left the boardroom were:
"You have to do what you love to be successful."

Your natural talents will lead you to pursuits that are creative
and risky or that involve methodical learning and less risk. With
either approach, the most successful leaders, executives, and entrepreneurs have found the thing that they love to do, and
because of it they have the passion and self-control to do it exceptionally well.

CHAPTER SIX

Emotional Awareness: Knowing Yourself and Others

Some people think only intellect counts: knowing how to solve problems, knowing how to get by, knowing how to identify an advantage and seize it. But the functions of intellect are insufficient without courage, love, friendship, compassion and empathy.

—DEAN KOONTZ, author of fiction who began writing as a strategy to survive a very difficult childhood

IN WESTERN CULTURE, we make distinctions between body and mind and between mind and heart. We like to think that there are two coexisting worlds, one of logic and reason and one of wild and uncontrolled emotions. Although it is true that emotion and thought activate different pathways in the brain, our reactions and our ability to cope integrate the two sides of ourselves. For example, in patients with brain damage, where only their capacity for emotional responses is impaired, their decision making is also affected.

One study in particular documented a patient who was highly rational but had lost the ability to feel emotions. On a particularly icy day he drove to the hospital in a fierce snowstorm to make his medical appointment when all of the other patients had cancelled that day. Because he didn't experience the emotion of fear, he simply got in his car and drove to the hospital. His IQ had not been affected by the brain damage, but when he was asked whether he would like to reschedule on Tuesday or Thursday, he simply could not make up his mind. Without his emotions, he had no preference to guide him in making a decision.[1] Emotion helps us reason.

> Those who don't pick up on the subtle emotional clues miss much of the content of what someone is really trying to convey.

Without a single word being exchanged, there is a subtle language of emotion that runs between the lines of every encounter we have in a day. Those who are aware of it can see that backdrop and examine the meanings that are both spoken and unspoken. In both professional and personal relationships, when someone is oblivious to the emotional tone of the situation, it can be like a frustrating itch in a hard-to-reach spot. Those who don't pick up on the subtle emotional clues miss much of the content of what someone is really trying to convey. Learning to be aware of emotions and then to make sense of them makes a person better at decision making, handling crises, and navigating the world of relationships.

Understated but defining, the language of emotions is one of the first ways we learn to communicate. Babies as young as ten months old learn what to make of a situation by watching their parents' faces and listening to the tone of their voices. One of the more famous studies of nonverbal communication examined what babies would do when they were placed on a "visual cliff" with their moms on the other side. The "cliff" was a glass-covered space with a deep end that seemed unsafe to cross. The babies would stop when they got to the edge of the "cliff" and look to their mother before going on. Out of the seventeen babies who saw mom looking fearful, not one of them ventured out over the cliff. In contrast, fourteen of the nineteen babies who saw mom smiling and looking calm scooted over the deep end without much fuss. In this experiment, the moms didn't say anything or use any gestures, but the babies read their moms' facial expressions.[2]

Although a baby can easily read the emotional tone of a situation, that skill can, unfortunately, get rusty with age. There are some who lose sight of this important piece of communication altogether. Yet an awareness of emotions is part of what distinguishes leadership that is great from that which is bad or indifferent. If you aren't tuned in to your own subtle emotions and to those of others, there likely will be frustration in the group, leaving a trail of angry people scratching their heads about why it's so unpleasant to be at work.

> If you aren't tuned in to your own subtle emotions and to those of others, there likely will be frustration in the group.

Emotions in the work setting have sometimes been given a bad rap. A good leader would make decisions based on cool-headed logic. We are expected to keep our personal problems at home. Apparently, the Puritan work ethic built the foundation for our "all work and no play" corporate culture. "If it were fun they wouldn't call it work" is a sad reflection of our acceptance of this outdated belief. And somehow the notion lingers that there should be a "work-life" balance, as if the two were mutually exclusive. But even the early research conducted by some of the first industrial psychologists found that emotion could not just be left at home.

The Hawthorne Effect

In the 1920s at the Western Electric Company in Cicero, Illinois, researchers descended on the Hawthorne plant with clipboards and surveys to measure productivity and happiness in response to such workplace environmental changes as increased lighting and shorter workdays. After changes were made, there was a noticeable rise in production, but a control group that didn't have any changes in its environment also improved productivity. It turned out that the workers' improved productivity was in response to the increased attention they were getting from the researchers. The plant workers felt like someone cared. It wasn't the physical conditions that made them happy; it was the social ones. This has become known as the Hawthorne Effect.

> The proper understanding and use of emotions can be critical in helping workers become more effective, better able to communicate, and simply happier at work.

After many dim decades, the light has finally been directed onto emotional intelligence, emotional competence, and authentic leadership as part of leadership language. Daniel Goleman popularized the concept in 1995 in his book *Emotional Intelligence*.[3] Now, there is a growing body of work in the emerging field of positive psychology, indicating that the proper understanding and use of emotions can be critical in helping workers become more effective, better able to communicate, and simply happier at work. Happier employees equal a happier (and more profitable) business. The emotional tone set by the leader is a large component of this happy business setting.

Leadership research tells us that the lack of interpersonal skills and the inability to adapt to the changing needs of co-workers are two principal derailment factors in executives' careers. When executives and managers misread what their people need, they are in danger of losing the "talent war" in an increasingly information-based world. Goals, visions, incentives, and bonuses are appreciated, but our basic human need is to have a supportive boss and good relationships with co-workers.

If the humanitarian aspect of this doesn't appeal to you, there's also a compelling bottom line. Thomas Wright, professor of organizational behavior at the University of Nevada, studied white-collar managers at large organizations and found that the happiness of employees accounts for between 10 and 25 percent of the variability in job performance.[4] Given a forty-hour work week, that could mean at least forty-eight minutes of productivity lost each day. Assuming an annual salary of $65,000 each for one hundred employees, improved well-being could account for a minimum of $650,000 in one year.

An organization's success has everything to do with its behavior toward people, both clients and employees. This all starts with leadership that is aware of the human, emotional side of the people who make up the workforce and the clients or customers. But what is *emotional awareness*, and how is it different from emotional intelligence?

Emotional Intelligence vs. Emotional Awareness

In an effort to expand the limited view of traditional concepts of intelligence, scientists researched and wrote about the idea of emotional intelligence. The work was done first by graduate student Wayne Payne in 1985, and later by professors John Mayer and Peter Salovey in the 1990s.[5] Their view of emotional intelligence is described as the ability to recognize emotion and then to understand and manage it.

Goleman's popular definition of emotional intelligence broadened the original understanding by also incorporating motivation, self-control, and social functioning. I address motivation in Chapter 4, self-control in Chapter 5, and social functioning in Chapter 7, but this chapter focuses on a person's ability to recognize and understand emotional issues, which is just one aspect of Goleman's description of emotional intelligence.

Emotional awareness is the ability to recognize one's own feelings and accurately read the feelings of others. The self-awareness component of the equation involves recognizing your own feelings and moods as they occur and realistically judging both how they affect your behavior and how that affects those around you. If you recognize you are feeling irritated because someone didn't finish a project as soon as you expected, and you know you have high, perhaps unreasonable, expectations, it gives you more options about what to do next, and it takes the sting out of the irritation. Now you have the choice of having a conversation that will get the results you both want. It leads to a sense of self-confidence and self-control when you understand your own feelings, strengths, and limitations. Self-awareness is the keystone of emotional intelligence. Even in the stoic rank-and-file of the U.S. Army, self-knowledge is listed as one of the eleven principles of leadership.

> *Emotional awareness* is the ability to recognize one's own feelings and accurately read the feelings of others.

Empathy is the other aspect of emotional awareness, and it is just as important as self-awareness, especially in leadership. Being able to understand and anticipate others' needs, feelings, and concerns is fundamental to emotional awareness. By understanding the feelings of others, you are better able to work with their emotional responses—something that catches many managers off guard. Empathy tunes you in to group dynamics, organizational culture, and the needs and expectations of customers and co-workers.

Many business leaders view empathy as the most necessary quality in good leadership, and studies have documented that empathy plays a part in both leader effectiveness and leader emergence in groups. In a qualitative study of twenty work groups in which no one was assigned a leadership role, those highest on several empathy scales emerged as informal leaders.[6] Those emergent leaders rose to the top because they understood the group members' emotional reactions to work events and therefore had the appropriate responses.

Group Conflict and Empathy

When leaders are emotionally synchronized with the rest of the group, there is a "resonance" and a shared experience and understanding of the task at hand.[7] Without such sensitivity, group members are left with feelings of disinterest, distraction, or worse, dissonance among themselves and their leader. A dissonant leader will just rub people the wrong way. Some of the conditions on *The Apprentice* make dissonant leadership more likely, simply because everyone in the group is an aggressive, driven, Type A personality. Oh, and by the way, they are all competing for one highly coveted slot, so making the leaders look good isn't their main motivation. Throw that factor into the mix along with the most challenging tasks the candidates have ever faced, and it's no wonder tempers flare.

When leaders are emotionally synchronized with the rest of the group, there is a "resonance" and a shared experience and understanding of the task at hand.

This was not the case when contestant Brian McDowell was the project manager for a motel renovation. Although it may not accurately reflect his leadership skills and is absolutely not indicative of his business success and savvy, the episode with Brian McDowell leading his team gives us a glimpse into group dissonance. Brian offered to take the reins on a task to renovate a motel on the south shore of Atlantic City, New Jersey.

Brian was mentioned in Chapter 5 for his entrepreneurial skills. He is used to acting independently. Of his own admission, he can be quite stubborn about the way to do things. It should also be mentioned that the task was fraught with impossible deadlines. With just $20,000, forty-eight hours, and a crew of four men and four women, each team was to renovate a musty, worn-down motel. Moldy carpets, exposed wiring, stained and broken bathroom fixtures, and discolored walls were the norm, and guests would be there to occupy the rooms in just two days. Tensions were high from the beginning and the strong personalities clashed. Brian took charge, which is what he does best—without realizing that the rest of the team was frustrated and disagreed with some of his decisions.

> Tensions were high from the beginning and the strong personalities clashed.

With just $20,000, forty-eight hours, and a crew of seven other competitors, Brian McDowell led his team in the renovation of a musty, worn-down motel.

Being on this show is a lot harder than it looks. Had Brian been too empathic and spent much more time dealing with the group's frustrations, he would never have completed the task; yet there were some missed moments when team members approached him and he wasn't sensitive to their concerns. For example, when the person in charge of the budget asked him to go over line items, he didn't do so and she then felt he didn't value her opinion and proceeded to sabotage him for the remainder of the project.

Brian had another talented Type A in his group, John Gafford, who became frustrated with the way Brian raised his voice at people on the team, and he approached him about it on the evening of the task. Brian's defense was that he couldn't help that his voice is loud. He just didn't realize how that was affecting the others and didn't see why he should act in a disingenuous way. In Brian's line of work, being independent, tough, and shrewd at negotiating, as well as standing firm, are what has made him such a success.

That night, however, exhausted and frustrated on the balcony of a dingy motel in Atlantic City, John was unable to get his point across and left angry and irritated. By the end of two days without sleep or much food, the whole group was in disarray: so annoyed and disenfranchised that their sour mood made the atmosphere of the Seaside Motel more like that of the Bates Motel. Guests checking into the motel lingered on the balconies to see why the "staff" was arguing in the parking lot.

In the end, both teams fell short of a completed renovation but managed to do an amazing amount, given the time and manpower constraints. The winner was decided by the online ratings the guests gave when they checked out in the morning. The unhappy mood that hung over Brian's motel likely influenced the ratings, and his team was informed of their loss in the boardroom. Their dissonance came with a price. Brian took full responsibility for the loss and was consequently fired.

> An emotionally aware leader is empathic, connected, and comfortable around others. The Machiavellian leader can have success, but the price will be high.

What can be learned from this example? Brian is extremely successful in the world of commerce; his tough-minded, inflexible persistence is what sets him apart. It is also the antithesis of what is needed to coexist in, much less, lead a group. His inclinations to seize opportunities and take huge risks are better done solo than under the constraints of an apprehensive group. An emotionally aware leader is empathic, connected, and comfortable around others. The Machiavellian leader can have success, but the price will be high.

As people become more educated, skilled, and talented in the workforce, this rigid position is increasingly tough to adopt. Of course, there are also times when a leader has to be tough-minded and nonemotional. Flexibility is required to know when and how much to use of the right emotion at the right time. A good leader even gets angry and frustrated. It is what is done next with those feelings that makes the difference between an approachable leader and one who is distant and removed.

The executive who sits in the corner office, out of touch with people, obsessively focused on the minutiae of paperwork and the bottom line, creates an emotionally chilly environment that can fuel discord and dissention. People end up feeling ignored, devalued, and disrespected, and that eventually breeds contempt and subtle rebellion.

A Leader from Boise

If the above is a picture of an out-of-touch and unexpressive leader, what does an emotionally aware leader look like? What are the results when someone is in tune with the people around him? One of the best examples *The Apprentice* has to offer is Troy McClain, from the very first season. Troy made an instant impression as the country boy from Boise, Idaho, who has dimpled good looks and an easy-going charm. He is principled and tough but engaging and mischievous at the same time.

Let's start with the results: Troy made it to the final four, which is impressive but all the more remarkable because he had no more than a high school education. He worked through high school and couldn't take time off for college because he was helping his single-parent mother take care of his hearing-impaired sister. Trump was impressed with Troy's ability to read a situation and to stay positive and poised under the most stressful situations.

It was immediately apparent that Troy had a pretty big heart. The small suite in which the contestants stay during the competition has everyone doubled up in closet-size bedrooms, and Troy's roommate was Sam Solovey. Sam was high-strung and tended to worry, and most people didn't have patience for him, as they were focused on the competition. Troy leaned over one day when Sam was nervous, gave him his cowboy hat, and talked him through a few moments of deep breathing and relaxation.

Troy's intuitive understanding for the feelings of others also impressed clients and made him a top negotiator on his team. About halfway through, the teams were given a list of five celebrities and were tasked to negotiate with each celebrity and develop an experience that could be auctioned off at Sotheby's for the Elizabeth Glaser Pediatric AIDS Foundation. That episode opened with Donald Trump's musing about how delicate negotiation is and that the most important factor is to figure out your opponent. Being perceptive of others isn't just humanitarian; it's good business practice.

Troy's team hopped in a cab to visit recording executive Russell Simmons, the founder of Def Jam Records. Con-testant Kwame Jackson was quite familiar with his work, so he did the talking. Kwame began his pitch, but Russell's look said, "Who are you and why are you wasting my time?" It was going south fast.

> Being perceptive of others isn't just humanitarian; it's good business practice.

Russell asked, "Are you a lawyer?" to which Kwame answered that he was a financial adviser. This brought another suspicious look from the "mogul of rap," but Kwame pressed on with the pitch, suggesting ideas that were quickly shot down. From the back of the group Troy said, "Russell, what we have in mind is something a person can experience with you."

Russell broke into a smile, and asked, "Where are you from?" They joked about his accent for a minute, and then Troy, sensing that they were aiming too high, proposed an evening with Russell where he would make that person feel "special." Russell loved the idea and they quickly closed the deal.

The next stop was a visit to the Fab Five from the TV program *Queer Eye for the Straight Guy*. Anticipating the need to quickly connect, Troy capitalized on the group's interest in critiquing straight guys. What better raw material than a straight country bumpkin? He deliberately took off his belt and hid it in his brief-case before they went in. The Fab Five were seated around a conference table as Troy walked in, announced that he was from Boise, and opened up his jacket. They instantly zeroed in on his missing belt and told him he "might as well be naked." After a good laugh, all five ended up agreeing to the first idea Troy presented.

Their final stop was designer Isaac Mizrahi, who was visibly put off when the project manager talked to him as if he had "never heard of an event like this before." He shot down two ideas, and the whole presentation was awkward and painful. Troy interjected, "How about we do a couple things with your chic ideas and then do a preview of your collection?" Isaac brightened and said, "Yes, how about that?" He jumped up, gave Troy a hug, and said, "*Mazel Tov!*"

In each situation, it was Troy's ability to put himself in the client's shoes, to empathize, and as Trump put it, to know his opponent, that saved the day. He focused on the celebrities and what they were communicating, both verbally and nonverbally.

> Empathy and self-awareness help leaders communicate more personably, give praise effectively, criticize constructively, and resolve conflicts more easily.

He was quick to grasp that they were busy and apprehensive about being approached and imposed upon, and he intuited that the offer would have to contain something that appealed to them and didn't take too much out of their busy schedule. Kwame later said that Troy was a great "closer," and that is because he listened and identified with his clients.

Empathy and self-awareness help leaders communicate more personably, give praise effectively, criticize constructively, and resolve conflicts more easily.

The next section, on self-awareness ("Insight Is Bliss"), examines the distinction between being reflective and being overwhelmed with personal feelings in a business setting. Before you can regulate your emotions and control the effect you have on others, you first have to become familiar with your internal world. A later section on empathy, "Interpreting Nonverbal Cues," will discuss the importance of body language, context, and a person's intonation, and will outline ways to effectively convey warmth and concern for another person. Being self-aware and in tune with what other people are feeling make you as appealing as, to quote Troy, "a virgin on prom night."

Insight Is Bliss

One of our key human strengths is self-awareness: the ability to recognize our strengths as well as our weaknesses. There is liberation in knowing who you are and in admitting, "Here I am, warts and all."

Insight is the lever that nudges you toward accountability, and it is the gold mine of psychotherapy. Abraham Maslow, an early pioneer in his focus on healthy personality qualities, wrote that ordinary individuals are often unaware of their desires and opinions whereas self-actualizing individuals are well aware of their impulses, opinions, and general reactions.[8]

An objective viewpoint allows you to engage in a "neutral self-reflection" that can be the end of getting caught off guard by overwhelming and destructive emotions.[9] There is nothing pleasant about being "hijacked" by powerful feelings, but it is not effective to simply ignore them, either. Keeping the lid tightly sealed and putting up a stoic front can be exhausting. It takes only an instant for the pot to boil over.

> There is nothing pleasant about being "hijacked" by powerful feelings, but it is not effective to simply ignore them, either.

If you have ever watched an episode of *The Apprentice*, you have seen heated emotions during the final scenes of the boardroom. You'll notice that the candidates who are verbal and informed about their opinions and feelings can keep calm amid the fray. In the midst of fighting, the emotionally aware person can step back from the situation and regroup. She can find a different approach or see another perspective. Detached self-reflection is like a third-party referee's keeping track of the score. It is entirely different from being overanalytical or intellectual, but it also doesn't involve getting swept away with the fervor of the moment.

With self-awareness, leaders can recognize what they are feeling on the spot, stay accurate about how this will influence what they are about to say or do next, and also know how it will probably affect others. Leadership is about communicating with other people, yet often interests diverge. This is painfully clear when you have to give someone negative feedback. You go in with a well-planned strategy, yet the other person doesn't respond the way you played it out in your mind. The person jabs back with "Well, but . . ." and "If you would have said that in the first place . . ." and "You should have. . . ." It can be a bit like stepping into the ring.

Your awareness of how you feel when you get attacked or blamed in a situation keeps you balanced and ultimately allows you to stay productive instead of throwing back wild punches. Likewise, effective leaders need to have the capacity to feel positive emotions even when those around them are experiencing frustration and defeat. They aren't caught off-guard by negativity and can stay on track, eventually guiding people toward resolution. That experience of getting though intense feelings without anyone feeling too badly bruised moves people from experiencing negative emotions to feeling more productive emotions.

Becoming More Self-Aware

We all come into this world with an emotional system that is both hard-wired and a product of our culture. Our culture and experience trains us to hide emotions or to express them in polite ways that may be a far cry from what we originally felt. This is especially true for men. It isn't that men are not as good at feeling and empathizing, it is just that, with the exception of anger, they are often trained to see emotions as "weak." But just as we get socialized to ignore feelings, we can learn to experience them again.

One of the first steps toward greater emotional awareness is to overcome the years of training and become accustomed to acknowledging emotional experiences. Patients often are healthier and more expressive after participating in group therapy because of the focus in such groups on strong emotions. Many facets of group therapy help heal, such as the development of trust and the ability to share experience, but one of the most useful components is simply learning the language of group therapy, which is prefaced with "I feel."

Group therapy may not be for everybody, but there are other ways to learn about feelings. Just getting in the habit of asking the question, "What am I feeling right now?" is a big start. Journaling is another way to become more self-aware. You can write about your dreams, about your past, about your family, about something that bothers you—the possibilities are endless.

Patients often are healthier and more expressive after participating in group therapy because of the focus in such groups on strong emotions.

After you gain familiarity with your internal world, start paying attention to your reactions to others. Carl Jung, the famous Swiss psychiatrist, put it very wisely when he said, "Everything that irritates us about others can lead to an understanding of ourselves."[10] Notice your feelings in reaction to people at your next boardroom meeting. When do you feel dominant, submissive, angry, serious, afraid?

Group therapy is also a fertile field for teasing out your reaction to others because you get to see that not everyone reacts the same way. Perhaps you have noticed this yourself. There can be someone in a meeting who really bothers you: he interrupts, he has an obnoxious opinion about everything, and he pretends to be the expert when he doesn't have half the training you have. But then you notice that other people actually like this guy's ideas! What's going on?

If you don't stop to examine the situation, you can get hijacked by feelings of anger, contempt, hatred, and hurt that people actually listen to this pompous guy. It may all be true; maybe he is pompous and controlling, but what is really important for self-awareness is the way *you* are reacting. You may be able to trace your reaction to an early experience that affected you, for instance. Using the example above, perhaps after some soul-searching you realize that you felt this way back in junior high school. There was a loud, domineering guy on the football team who managed to completely snow the coach. You felt frustrated because you were never given a chance—and this is the exact feeling you are having now. Recognizing that reference point is liberating and powerful because it means you don't have to be blinded by those feelings.

> Ignorance of the self is viewed by Zen Buddhism as the source of human suffering; self-knowledge is considered a key to enlightenment.

Once you get the hang of it, you can relate just about any feeling that you are having to something within yourself. If you have a negative reaction to someone who is "loud and obnoxious," maybe you aren't speaking up enough for yourself. If you can't stand someone who is overly dramatic, maybe life is becoming too safe and predictable for you, yet you are afraid to rock the boat. The clues about our reactions to people can usually be found in some aspect of our own life: something from our past, a difficulty we are struggling with, a fear about the future. By sorting it all out, we not only gain control over our emotional responses to other people, we also acquire insight that may help us solve our problem. Ignorance of the self is viewed by Zen Buddhism as the source of human suffering; self-knowledge is considered a key to enlightenment.

Troy McClain is self-aware; it is something he does automatically. During Troy's final boardroom, he and Kwame were the final two left on their team. This boardroom paired a Harvard MBA (Kwame) with a high school graduate (Troy).

The facts of the assignment were rehashed and the two candidates fought it out in a gentlemanly way. In the end, Trump said that he was impressed with Troy and that he would be a great success, but felt that Kwame had an edge owing to his education. Troy was proud of Trump's endorsement and also quite happy with how far he had made it, yet he had a slight sense of sadness that he couldn't quite identify.

Troy said in later interviews that he realized Donald Trump had been a powerful mentor whom he did not want to let down.

Troy realized that having a mentor was especially important to him. He decided that, although he had always been busy caring for family and didn't attend college, education was now something he was going to make a priority.

Someone less able to reflect on his feelings would be more likely to ignore that slight bit of sadness. Without that ability to figure out why this experience had such a hold on him, he wouldn't have bounced back so quickly, nor would he have taken positive steps to finish college. With practice, you too can develop the ability to recognize your feelings. Take the time to identify what you are feeling right now and then relate that to past feelings. Once you are familiar with your internal world, there are other skills that can help you regulate powerful feelings; these are discussed in the next section.

Regulating the Emotions

When it comes to anger and other negative feelings, the popular notion is that you should let it all out—like opening a steam valve, this will relieve the tension of the feeling. Sigmund Freud's idea of catharsis led people to believe that if the feeling was acknowledged and expressed, this would relieve its negative effects. Research on the role of emotions in the disease process has indicated that, although it is important to acknowledge anger, simply expressing and venting anger with abandon actually intensifies it.

> Research on the role of emotions in the disease process has indicated that, although it is important to acknowledge anger, simply expressing and venting anger with abandon actually intensifies it.

The early years of research into Type A behavior uncovered a personality pattern that contributed, along with lifestyle factors like smoking and diet, to heart disease. It was originally thought that the Type A person bottled up intense, angry feelings, which contributed to strains on their heart. After years of study, however, that notion was revised; both suppressing and expressing negative emotions contribute to poor health. Recent research at Johns Hopkins University has confirmed that medical students who express their anger, who are irritable, and who complain without working on resolutions are five times more likely to have a heart attack than their calmer classmates.[11]

If someone is angry and she vents, or even worse, takes it out physically, those actions fuel the fire and make the person angrier as she reinforces the feelings through her statements.[12] She may eventually wear herself out, but she is also more likely to repeat that negative behavior the next time. So what are you supposed to do if it is unhealthy both to suppress and to express negativity? Instead of venting in a way that doesn't lead to resolution, positively manage your emotions.

For example, when it comes to anger, there are three stances or responses that you can take: aggressive (venting); passive (suppressing); or assertive.

An aggressive response is one in which you dominate a situation or person in a forceful and disrespectful way, which ignores another person's feelings or takes advantage of a situation. Passivity turns that anger inward, where it festers and reduces your self-esteem. Assertiveness is simply speaking the truth in a way that is respectful of others and reasonable enough that it doesn't just incite more anger. Learning to be assertive is a way to manage and express negative feelings to reduce the intensity rather than fuel more negative emotion.

> Learning to be assertive is a way to manage and express negative feelings to reduce the intensity rather than fuel more negative emotion.

Discriminating statements can also help manage negative feelings. As we navigate through the day, there are some times when everything seems to go well and some times when nothing seems to go right. We have little successes and failures throughout the day. What you tell yourself in these situations makes the difference between feeling overwhelmed and hopeless or in control of the situation. For example, following some kind of setback—say you failed to make a sale because you didn't have time to research your client's needs—what you tell yourself about why it happened will make a difference. If you put it in unconditional terms (e.g., "I am a failure"), you will have negative feelings about the situation. A discriminative statement produces fewer negative feelings of being overwhelmed (e.g., "I fail when I don't make sure I have adequate time before I take on a new project").

We have all known some people who have a way of managing their emotions much more effectively than others. Many theories have been advanced about why this is so; the field of positive psychology has examined ways of thinking that lead to successful management of the emotions. Those who are self-aware, who don't shy away from tough emotions, and who don't get bowled over by them, either, use what is called discriminative thinking. This way of thinking reduces the tendency to turn a failure into a catastrophe.

> **Part of emotional awareness is having the ability to regulate strong feelings (like guilt, self-hatred, sadness, and anger) through the statements you make to yourself.**

Part of emotional awareness is having the ability to regulate strong feelings (like guilt, self-hatred, sadness, and anger) through the statements you make to yourself. Instead of thinking, "I am a failure," try "I fail when . . . I am not prepared, I am preoccupied with problems, I stay up all night working on a project, or I take on too many things at once." Not only is this thinking a buffer against global negative feelings, it also has the potential for you to make improvements in future situations.

The tools of optimistic thinking lead to effective emotional management as well. Remember, there is a difference between self-reflection and rumination. *Rumination* means, literally, "chewing the cud," as does a cow or sheep that gnaws on food. It is an unattractive, but descriptive analogy of going over and over in your mind a negative or troubling thought, without making any forward movement.

Women are twice as likely to suffer from depression as men, and one of the contributing factors is thought to be the ruminative way they tend to contemplate problems.[13] This rumination amplifies negative feelings. Men, on the other hand, tend to be more action-oriented and don't spend as much time mulling things over. The goal for both men and women is to be more self-aware and self-reflective, yet not to get into a rut of overanalyzing.

> Optimistic thinking involves looking at problems as temporary, specific, and nonpersonal.

Thinking about an emotion with an optimistic style steers you away from lingering over troubling negative feelings. Optimistic thinking involves looking at problems as temporary, specific, and nonpersonal. In Troy's example, he was feeling a little bit sad. If he had been a pessimist, his thinking might have gone as follows: "I am a loser for not having an education" (personal); "I have always been at a disadvantage because I didn't go to college" (global); and "I will never have a chance like this again" (permanent).

Troy is a natural optimist, so it never occurred to him to think in such a damaging way, but even a hardened pessimist can learn to rephrase thoughts about setbacks, even if it feels a bit contrived at first. The optimistic explanation Troy gave for his situation was: "I was always busy working to help out my Mom and my sister, so there were more important things to do than college" (external instead of personal); "I have always been successful at everything I try; it is just that Kwame had more education this time" (specific instead of global); and "Not having that degree held me back this time, but I am enrolling in classes as soon as I get back" (temporary instead of permanent).

Thinking in this way capitalizes on the best natural tendencies of both genders. You take the time to acknowledge a feeling, but the way that you think about it is productive and action-oriented.

The usefulness of this thinking has been demonstrated to help lift depression. It also helps you learn how to regulate emotions without being swept away or overpowered.

Here's a final word about emotional regulation and using cognitive tools to help manage feelings: there's a difference between naïve, "hope for the best" optimism and positive behavioral coping. Optimism isn't just an attempt to eliminate the negative and accentuate the positive. Though there are times when it is best to inhibit a negative feeling, the ability to disclose and acknowledge difficult feelings leads to healthy coping. Accentuating the positive is a useful outlook on life and offers many physical, mental, and interpersonal benefits. Negative feelings aren't suppressed; they are recognized and then redirected.

When it comes to leadership and management, emotional awareness helps you stay on track when there is interpersonal conflict or a counterproductive work relationship. Those you lead will sense your comfort with your own feelings, and this, in turn, will lend credibility and make you more approachable and more comfortable with others' conflicts. Specifically, it will help you give constructive criticism, resolve conflicts, and communicate better—all in a tone of acceptance and competence.

Learning to Show More Empathy

Books that teach people how to manipulatively "read" other people or know when someone is lying are popular business material, yet being "empathic" is looked on as soft and sentimental. The truth is that being empathic is what allows you to "read" people. As discussed in the "Insight is Bliss" section, self-awareness is the ability to recognize your own feelings and moods and then judge realistically how they affect your behavior. Social awareness, or empathy,

> **Social awareness, or empathy, is the ability to understand the feelings of others and judge how that affects their behavior.**

is the ability to understand the feelings of others and judge how that affects their behavior. Empathy involves understanding other people's perspectives—sensing their feelings and concerns and how that affects their needs.

Empathy is a cornerstone of social skills—something that is crucial for getting by in the world, but it isn't customarily taught in school. It is the topic of many parent-teacher conferences and is an undertone in every grade we attend, yet it isn't always addressed openly. Training for teaching such social skills and developing emotional intelligence has been demonstrated to have a significant impact and is slowly leaking into the curriculum as we begin to realize just how important these skills are to people's overall well-being.

One of the saddest by-products of a lack of empathy is the teasing and bullying that has, at its worst, culminated in shocking school violence. Although teasing isn't the only culprit in the rise of school violence, it does have a prominent place. The picture that emerged after the Columbine shootings was that Eric Harris and Dylan Kleibold had both been outcasts who had been cruelly teased and bullied for years.

When the New York City Schools conducted a Resolving Conflict Program in 1988, teachers used various skills training to help develop empathy.[14] The results were exciting: more empathy, more cooperation, less class violence, and improved communication skills. Clearly, when social skills and empathy are taught and emphasized, the result is a better school environment, both socially and academically.

A leader with empathy is better able to resolve conflicts, is more adept at motivating and inspiring the team, and fosters a more cooperative work environment. The ability to recognize and respond accordingly to someone's feelings and concerns is what makes a person approachable and dependable—someone you would want to work for.

Is empathy inborn or is it something that is learned? Neuropsychological studies tell us that if a mother is "in tune" with her baby's needs, the part of the brain that has to do with warmth, relationships, and empathy is activated.[15] Because the mother is responding accurately to what her child needs (a bottle, a smile, a nap, etc.), the child will also develop empathy. Upon further examination, it turns out that although this is true, the picture is slightly more complicated by the personality of the baby.

Researchers also have noticed that some babies magnetically attract adults. They smile more, coo more, cry less, and engage the adults around them. It appears to be a two-way reaction: yes, a responsive mother helps foster warmth, trust, and empathy in a child, but some babies are born with outgoing charm and bring out the best in the adults around them. As with most of the personality traits, it turns out to be a complex mix of genetics and surroundings that contributes to this interpersonal skill.

Regardless of your own genetic and social influences, you can learn to be more empathic. Active engagement with someone in an empathic way, even if it at first feels contrived, will begin an upward spiral of optimism and understanding. Others will respond to your attempts at empathy and their responses will fuel further action on your part.

When it comes to leading people, showing empathy doesn't mean having an unconditional positive regard. Without some teeth, this type of leadership sets a tone of mediocrity where everyone is praised indiscriminately. Empathy allows a leader to understand those around him and make more sensitive and informed decisions. Most of the skills that encourage empathy are easy to practice.

> Showing empathy doesn't mean having an unconditional positive regard. Without some teeth, this type of leadership sets a tone of mediocrity where everyone is praised indiscriminately.

The most obvious empathy-building skill is that of listening. If you listen with the intention of gaining a better understanding of the other person, you have to suspend judgment, ask lots of questions to clarify, and then demonstrate that you understand what was shared.

Another useful skill is that of "mirroring." Having a feeling mirrored back creates a powerful sense of confidence and well-being. Mirroring isn't parroting back what other people say; it is simply responding in kind. When Troy approached a nervous Sam, he acknowledged Sam's anxiety and talked about staying calm. He was on Sam's wavelength. He didn't lecture or try to cajole him out of it; he simply responded to Sam's nervousness.

Empathy-building skills also involve understanding nonverbal communication. In the 1970s, Dr. Albert Mehrabian, with a background in engineering and natural science, found that verbal communication accounts for only about 7 percent of a message. About 38 percent is conveyed in the tone of voice; the rest, 55 percent, comes from nonverbal language like gestures, postures, and facial expressions.[16] Some people are just naturally adept at reading nonverbal meanings, but Dr. Mehrabian's research makes it possible for anyone to understand the emotional undertones of someone's message.

Interpreting Nonverbal Cues

There are three primary dimensions for understanding nonverbal cues: immediacy, animation, and dominance. *Immediacy* refers to closeness. If someone is leaning forward, she generally likes you, and if she leans back, she is uncertain or hesitant. Eye contact and touching also communicate the degree of contact someone desires. If you see that someone isn't making eye contact and is sitting far away, you can guess that the other person is not at ease.

> **If you see that someone isn't making eye contact and is sitting far away, you can guess that the other person is not at ease.**

Animation is another dimension of nonverbal language. When someone is interested and lively about a subject, he is more high-energy and dynamic. A flat tone communicates a lack of interest. If someone has that sparkle in his eye, a high-pitched tone, and animated facial expression, those communicate his interest about a topic and provide a cue in how to respond.

Nonverbal cues can also transmit information about the balance of power in a relationship, a dimension Mehrabian termed *dominance.* Cues in this category contain information about relative status and importance. A person of higher status will have a more relaxed posture when she is interacting with someone of lower status. The high-status person tends to have more space, such as a large corner office, and more "barriers," such as assistants and secretaries. You can begin to empathize with people by understanding these nonverbal cues, and if you want to put someone at ease, consider how much dominance is established simply by virtue of the physical surroundings. A dominant or forceful tone may be overkill.

One final word of caution about reading nonverbal cues: they are not definitive. The best way to check your hypothesis is to ask. For example, if someone has his arms crossed, it could be a sign that he is creating a distance and closing himself off to the interaction. Upon asking, however, you may find out that the room is cold and he is attempting to stay warm. The skills of empathy, after all, are an attempt to understand another person, not a means to manipulate and mind-read.

> **Empathy and emotional awareness go hand in hand when it comes to creating "resonant" leadership and group cohesiveness.**

Empathy and emotional awareness go hand in hand when it comes to creating "resonant" leadership and group cohesiveness. Neither of these qualities will hurt you in personal relationships, either. For example, empathy is also key to successful marriages. These skills can be used in a wide variety of interpersonal situations, but the last section of this chapter, "The Guide for Emotionally Aware Management," has specific guidance for leading with emotional awareness.

Women, Competition, and Emotion

Since we are talking about empathy, emotional awareness, and interpersonal skills, you may wonder whether women have an advantage in this arena. Common sense might say yes, but empathy is a skill that both men and women can use help in refining. Each gender (in a general sense, though this doesn't apply to all individuals) has its advantages and disadvantages in the workplace.

Many of the contestants on *The Apprentice* wonder why there is so much fighting among the women when they are together on a team, whereas the men seem to get along more often. Both season one and season two teams were divided along gender lines, and both times the women's group had more interpersonal troubles. It didn't typically affect them in the number of wins and losses, but there was a noticeable difference in the way they related to each other.

Are women more emotional than men in the business world? That's the question Matt Lauer posed to a panel of experts on a segment of the *Today* show after five women in a row were fired on season one of *The Apprentice*. The first four candidates fired were all men, but the show aired quite a few clips of bitter arguments on the women's team.

Indeed, that first season had some interesting drama. The women had heated arguments, even when they were on their winning streak. The same pattern continued on season two, when teams were again divided into men and women. The boardrooms got particularly heated, and those personal differences flared up again back in the suite. Cliques formed on the women's team and, along with it, resentments.

So Matt Lauer asked George Ross and Carolyn Kepcher, Donald Trump's top advisers, his question about gender and emotion in business. Carolyn and George observe the team competitions and advise Trump about the candidates' performances. Matt pointed out that when students in an MBA program were polled, their consensus was that the women on the show were not typical of "real" women in business. Carolyn commented that the women on season one used their sexuality and that she sees that in the business world also. George suggested that women may be a little more emotional, but that he didn't see that difference in the business world.

Research suggests that men and women do have some genuine differences in terms of expressing emotions, and that would naturally spill over into the work world.[17] The differences in *The Apprentice* setting are heightened because the men and women also live together for six weeks in very close quarters. They share kitchen space, sleep two to a tiny room, and have very limited contact with outsiders.

This arrangement has caused trouble for the women. Though women are less confined by gender-specific stereotypes than in decades past, they have generally been socialized to be nurturing and to pay attention to relationships, while men have typically been encouraged to make things, be active and competitive, and excel in sports. As much as we may try to reduce the gender gap, a visit to many schoolyards during recess will reveal the differences. The boys will be hotly involved in a loud and boisterous sport, absorbed in one thing: beating each other. They playfully tease, argue bitterly over a play, and then quickly get back to the game without so much as a "sorry." The girls compete in a very different way. They often stop a game if someone isn't happy; they'll discuss and reason and try to make sure everyone is OK. Girls talk to each other face-to-face and try to gain consensus; boys play hard shoulder-to-shoulder without much dialogue.

Ask any teacher whether the boys or girls are more "polite" and "well behaved." Watch as a crowd of boys sits down in a group. They will bump, push, and jostle for a spot. Girls will sit quietly and make sure that everyone has a spot. Many of today's parents echo the sentiment: they give their kids gender-neutral toys or get the girls to play with a tool set and the boys with a kitchen set. They are dismayed that their girls still clamor for a Barbie Doll and their boys turn a stick into a make-believe gun or sword. It seems to be (as usual) a little bit nature and a little bit nurture—and even marketing gets into the act. When you walk down the Toys 'R' Us aisles, you will

> When you walk down the Toys 'R' Us aisles, you will know when you are in the girls section: it will be pink and have every kind of baby doll imaginable.

know when you are in the girls section: it will be pink and have every kind of baby doll imaginable. The boys section will be bold blues, reds, and yellows, with lots of tools, vehicles, and action sets.

When we enter the work world, a little of this influence lingers. During season one, Omarosa Manigault Stallworth came into the game with a "masculine" strategy that she was going to compete and didn't care to make friends with the other women. It made sense because the only person she had to impress was Donald Trump. The other women were competitors, so why bother to fake it? One explanation for the resulting discord toward Omarosa is that the rest of the women sensed something amiss; although they were quite competitive, they wanted everyone to get along and to bond as a team. Even in competing for the Apprenticeship, they were compelled to smooth out the relationships.

That isn't to say that relationships aren't ever important to men and always are to women. Sam Solovey was very concerned

During season one, Omarosa Manigault Stallworth came into the game with a "masculine" strategy.

about his bonds with his teammates and staged a "sit-in" in the hall because he came into the suite and no one greeted him at the door. Many men and many women don't fit neatly into the categories of masculine and feminine. Gender roles are broad and stereotyped and don't ever adequately describe one individual. They do, however, explain overall group behavior; in this case, they may suggest why the women had such a hard time coexisting even though they were unbeaten in the competition. Men tend to bond during competition; women can struggle with rivalry (especially when they also have to live together!) because they also want everyone to get along.

Women also tend to express more emotions. Research hints at a genuine gender difference that appears to be a result of socialization. Physical measures of emotional responses by infant boys and girls to the sound of another baby crying indicate that boys are more distressed and more emotionally aroused than infant girls, but that the results are reversed and the gap widened with each year of growth, with boys becoming less sensitive to others' distress over time.[18] This isn't necessarily a good or healthy thing for men, who frequently have trouble expressing their feelings. Often their emotions get channeled into the one feeling they are allowed to express—anger. By the time they compete on *The Apprentice*, the men are generally more comfortable with competition, anger, and confrontation. During the show, it often appears that women are combative in the boardroom but in a more aggressive than assertive way.

When the women's emotions get heated, the perception is that they are out of control. For many women, learning to express anger in a relaxed, comfortable, and assertive manner can overcome the tension they feel between wanting to compete and feeling uncomfortable with anger and conflict.

Men and women have different disadvantages in business when it comes to emotional expression. Many men are constricted in their emotional repertoire as they attempt to be strong and silent[19]—there are countless social forces teaching them to be "cool." But there is a price to pay for living up to this impossible standard. Men can improve both their work and their personal lives through emotional awareness and empathy.

Women have been socialized to thrive on relationships rather than on power over others. They may focus on others at the expense of meeting their own needs, which can turn into passive aggressiveness, manipulation, and resentment. Women, however, are great communicators: girls learn to speak and develop bigger vocabularies earlier, and that pays off later. They can become more comfortable with competition by learning how to better resolve conflicts with others. By becoming more aware of what they are feeling, they can learn to express anger in direct and productive ways.

For both men and women, becoming more emotionally aware of both their own feelings and the feelings of others will enhance their success in the business world. The following section elaborates on the suggestions made earlier for developing those skills.

The Guide for Emotionally Aware Management

Initial Steps

Effective leaders know how to align their emotions with their groups' emotions, and thus create "resonance" and shared understanding. This alignment means sharing both negative and positive emotions. Effective leaders are comfortable with a whole range of emotions and can help others move from experiencing negative emotions to feeling more productive emotions.

Leadership style should fit the situation and the person. Sometimes it must be very clear, direct, and authoritarian; at other times it should focus on relationships. The following suggestions for increasing emotional awareness will help you tune in to those around you and gain sensitivity in selecting the right style for the job.

- **Be authoritative, not authoritarian**. With the exception of the Armed Forces and crisis situations, when employees are expected to do it "because I told you so," being forced into compliance without an explanation generally creates dissatisfaction. People want to have a feeling of control. The best way to prevent misunderstandings, create a sense of trust, and reduce uncertainty is to give clear and specific information. Knowledge is power, but to hold on to it doesn't give you any edge.

- **Provide social and emotional support**. This is an essential part of the work environment: something that has been recognized in the research since the days of the Hawthorne Effect. Things like family days, rituals to celebrate success, and willingness to revise policies to reduce stress are all ways to enliven the social atmosphere. People need times to come together and socialize; it is a mistake to expect "all work and no play." A popular test to assess career choice is the Strong-Campbell Interest Inventory. It compares your values and interests to others in various career fields. The test matches your interests to the job, but also to the interests of the people you will work with. The test, available in most counseling centers at colleges and universities, recognizes that vocational satisfaction is related to social support.

- **Give sensitive feedback**. Feedback is perhaps one of the most powerful tools of an emotionally aware leader.[20] The transformative influence of a valid critique can be astounding. I have seen it done well, and it turned an angry, disgruntled, unhappy employee into a cheerful co-worker who was a delight to be around. The "Further Steps" section will have some suggestions for managing your own anxiety in this and other interpersonal situations. What does good feedback sound like? Donald Trump is pretty skillful at giving feedback. He articulates the drawbacks of someone's personality without the benefits of psychological testing. He is specific—for example, he has told contestants they were too emotional, too inexperienced, or too conservative in taking risks. He offers a solution and makes his communication personal; and believe it or not, he can even be sensitive, although he has given many *Apprentice* candidates withering criticisms. He has given heartfelt advice and has let candidates know how impressed he is with their overall performance, even if they failed on a task.

Further Steps

- **What you communicate**. Research indicates that the greatest source of interpersonal discord in both work and family is communication difficulties. Helpful communication consists of using language that is understandable, responds to the primary message, and stays positive instead of focusing on negative aspects of the conversation. Good eye contact, facial animation, and matching the tone of voice to the person you are talking to send helpful nonverbal messages. Nonhelpful communication consists of interrupting, giving advice, blaming, lecturing, and being patronizing. Nonverbal cues that are unhelpful include frowning, crossing your arms, looking away, and using a harsh tone of voice.

- **Conflict resolution and anxiety management**. For some people, conflict and confrontation are extremely uncomfortable. This discomfort can sabotage your efforts to be a good listener and sabotage your attempts to put good communication skills into practice. A few things can help manage your tension: (1) listen first before you jump in, (2) give the other person time to speak, and (3) practice objectivity. Ask yourself if there are good reasons for your reaction or if you are jumping to conclusions.[21] Also, ask questions to clarify rather than ones that are judgmental or hostile. Here are a few questions you can ask yourself that will help identify your anxiety:

Am I uncomfortable with a particular person or situation?

Is there something I am doing to avoid the situation?

Do I always have to be in control?

Going Beyond

Although this book is about personality strengths rather than leadership styles, an emotionally aware leader is able to adapt and put on the right leadership hat for the right situation. There are many leadership styles out there, each with its own benefits.

A *visionary* leader moves people toward a shared dream; this style is appropriate when a new direction is needed.[22] An *affiliative* leader focuses on connection and harmony; use this style in a stressful work environment or when there are divisions among team members. A *commanding* leader is abrupt and directive, and has to make tough and unpopular decisions; sometimes this is the only style that will work when a company is headed for serious trouble—it can shock people out of unproductive work habits and complacency.

You can see in these three examples that there is variability in leadership styles, and one leadership style isn't superior to another. Indeed, rigidly adhering to one style creates dissonance. For example, a rigid and emotionally unaware leader will miss the signs calling for a particular style, but an emotionally skilled leader will find the right style for the given situation.

One final aspect of a warm charismatic leader is an ability to foster relationships and to be personable. Chapter 7 explains the importance of being personable and paying attention to relationships.

CHAPTER SEVEN

Sociability and Relationships: No Entrepreneur Is an Island

Without relationships, no matter how much wealth, fame, power, prestige and seeming success by the standards and opinions of the world one has, happiness will constantly elude him.

> —SIDNEY MADWED, public speaker and teacher of motivation and stress management; member of The National Speakers Association and the International Speakers Association and member and poet laureate of The New England Speakers Association

A CONVERSATION with a typical *Apprentice* contestant is usually animated, energized, and loud. Indeed, part of the profile of a typical candidate for *The Apprentice* is being extroverted and liking people. This type of person can't stay quiet, often got in trouble when she was young for talking too much in class, and gets to know the wait staff and probably a few fellow diners whenever she goes to a restaurant. Of course, the pool of applicants for a reality show is a skewed sample. That is, the fact that these successful contestants are all so extroverted and outgoing could just be that they are the type of person who wants to appear on national television. After all, someone who is introverted or uninterested in other people wouldn't entertain the idea of being on camera. Nevertheless, there is much to be learned from this select group of people.

Perhaps that outgoing manner and interest in relating to others *The Apprentice* candidates have feeds their overall tendency to be optimistic; for them, this friendly way of looking at others contributes to a positive mood and a hopeful outlook on life. What appears to be a strong association between friendliness and happiness, with relationships being a strong predictor of mental health and well-being, has been substantiated elsewhere. For example, when social psychologists ask people what makes life most meaningful, their responses are overwhelmingly uniform: being loved and appreciated. As a matter of fact, people rank their relationships with family, friends, and co-workers above job satisfaction and financial security.[1] Being sociable and forming relationships with other people are important, both at home and at work.

> Although it may never be overtly mentioned in a performance review, poor relationships with others can be a deal breaker.

You would never know it from the heated attacks in the boardroom each week of *The Apprentice*, but the contestants are also forming strong bonds. Yes, it may not look that way as you watch the show, but bonding is one of the most powerful things that happens on the show. If a contestant has trouble establishing relationships, he may not be the first, second, or even third person to be fired, but it is highly unlikely that he will make it to the end. Sociability is an important business skill. Although it may never be overtly mentioned in a performance review, poor relationships with others can be a deal breaker. And sociability is a personality characteristic of contestants on other reality shows that have nothing to do with leadership or business. A person who is ill at ease with relationships, either at home or at work, is likely to experience other performance-related problems as well. Social skills affect everything from the bottom line to our general well-being.

Make Two New Friends and Call Me in the Morning

Did you know that good relationships can actually contribute to your health? People who are isolated and have few social contacts do, in fact, increase their risk for premature death. Amazingly, the health risks associated with loneliness are greater than those connected with either smoking or obesity.[2] That means you can eat that cheeseburger—just share it with a friend!

The Apprentice candidates are young, so their overall health is good anyway, but they will be more likely to enjoy good health as they get older. They are like big Labrador puppies bumping about the room, knocking things over in their eagerness to be close to people. They have the ability to genuinely care about the strangers they come in contact with every day; indeed, their interest in people is partly what makes them so appealing. It is easy enough to dismiss their outgoing personalities as attention-seeking, needy, or even too intrusive. They will be the ones holding up that supermarket line you're in while they have a leisurely chat with not only the cashier but also the bagger. An introvert will see the extrovert's energy as a little too much to handle. I had a very sociable godmother like this—extremely talkative, prattling on to anyone who would listen; after one of her visits, my grandmother would exclaim, "Oh, she wears me out!"

Though sociability doesn't come naturally to those of a more solitary nature, the ability to relate to strangers is a useful weapon in any battle against depression. Intimate relationships certainly give comfort, but the ability to connect with strangers has a lot more to offer than you might suspect. Being sociable contributes to good physical health and overall happiness, as well as better adjustment to life.

> Intimate relationships certainly give comfort, but the ability to connect with strangers has a lot more to offer than you might suspect.

Alfred Adler, a psychologist from Germany and one of Freud's inner circle, came to disagree with the importance Freud placed on the internal mechanisms of the psyche. He believed that the source of good mental health is social interest.[3] *Social interest* describes how active and vital you feel you are as part of the human race.

Mental health is positively affected by maintaining close contacts with other people. For example, marriage is a strong predictor of happiness: 40 percent of married adults call themselves "very happy," as opposed to 23 percent of their unmarried counterparts.[4] Although many contestants on the show are not married, relating to other people is what makes them tick. They form close bonds and some still talk to each other every day, even years after their episode has aired. They have genuine interest in other people, love conversation, and regard relationships with others as what makes them come to life.

Effective Leaders Are Sociable

So, do extroversion and sociability really contribute to success in the "real" business world? We seem to intuitively recognize the value of socializing or "networking" in business affairs, but there is also evidence for the importance of good social skills in regard to leadership. For example, there are steep monetary and emotional costs when companies fail to find the right person for a leadership job. When a new executive is brought in, with much enthusiasm and anticipation, because of her experience, professionalism, and technical skill, it is disappointing and frustrating to see her turn out to be a "disaster," as Donald Trump would say. Technical skills may get someone the job, but personal and interpersonal skills lead to eventual success or failure.

Some of the most telling research on the effect that sociability has on performance comes from the world of sports. The link between team unity and sports performance has been well established. When sports teams feel solidarity and cohesion, they are more likely to play well. But any kind of team can be united in a task or defined simply by the members' relationships with each other; both types of cohesion ensure that members achieve common performance goals. Interestingly, in one analysis of forty-six studies of team performance, it was social cohesion, rather than task cohesion, that predicted better performance. Likewise, coach-athlete relationships are important to team performance. Collaborations that include mutual trust, cooperation, respect, and commitment are more likely to produce team camaraderie and success on the playing field. But when coaches and their athletes have conflicts and power struggles, it negatively affects team unity and individual performance.[5] Off the field, the same picture emerges: poor relationships produce poor results, and quality relationships yield quality results.

> Technical skills may get someone the job, but personal and interpersonal skills lead to eventual success or failure.

> Collaborations that include mutual trust, cooperation, respect, and commitment are more likely to produce team camaraderie and success on the playing field.

The traits that make up successful leadership include general intelligence, initiative, assertiveness, competitiveness, self-control, stress tolerance, enthusiasm, and *extroversion*.[6] Taken together, these qualities constitute a person who is self-confident, outgoing, and sociable. Leadership style aside, the quality of relationships between supervisors and employees predicts either positive or negative outcomes. And these quality relationships are most easily developed through sociability. Sociability is the lubricant that leaders use to build team cohesion.

The Price of Social Neglect

The next time you feel too rushed to say "Good Morning" and take a little time to chat, stop right there. Think about some of the headaches you could avoid with a cheerful "Hi!" Ignoring or feeling superior to staff, regardless of rank, is a mistake no wise leader makes. Co-workers who feel neglected eventually retaliate. An unapproachable leader who feels himself higher or superior to others will soon pay the price for that distance. When people think they are being treated unfairly they get back in subtle and not-so-subtle ways to remedy the "injustice."[7] They may take extra-long breaks, call in sick when they are healthy, spread gossip, damage equipment, and sabotage projects. Like Dolly Parton, Jane Fonda, and Lily Tomlin, who gave their boss rat poison in the movie *Nine to Five*, they will gang up on you—and it could get ugly. An employee who feels poorly treated finds a way to get revenge, ranging from bad-mouthing and backstabbing to whistleblowing and litigation.

In the first season, when *The Apprentice* candidates were pressed for time during a task to sell pallets of Trump Ice, the team that managed to get to know a little about their potential buyers won the task by a large margin. In the boardroom, George pointed out that one team's "closer" came in with a sales pitch about what the team could do for the restaurant. The other team's "closer" chatted with the restaurant owners, asked them a few questions, and worked his magic building good relations—and his team won the task.

> The extroverted and sociable leader has genuine rapport and evident, true human interest in others, even when there have to be tough directives.

Not every situation calls for a leader to be democratic and collaborative, and not every task includes teamwork and communication. But an affiliative leader knows how to boost morale, nurture relationships, and demonstrate true empathy.[8] The extroverted and sociable leader has genuine rapport and evident, true human interest in others, even when there have to be tough directives. An important component of effective leadership is the ability to be strong and directive while retaining "social interest."

Indeed, leadership is an art of persuading people, especially in today's workplace where there is no longer a rigid hierarchy of superiors and subordinates. Over the past three or four decades, there has been a shift from dominant central leaders to shared power and follower involvement. Companies have to work a little harder to retain their talent, owing to increased career opportunities, globalization of business activities, and expanded dependence on information technology. The times of authoritarian bosses are long gone. Ironically, although the workforce still needs leaders with good people skills, most young talent is selected on the basis of technical skills. People can end up in a leadership role before they gain the maturity and perspective to manage others.

The Runner-Up with Charm

You can become better at relationships, even if you are an introvert. But before you aspire to improve your social skills, it helps to know what a personable leader looks like. Season one of *The Apprentice* presented a great example of an extroverted leader.

> Before you aspire to improve your social skills, it helps to know what a personable leader looks like.

Kwame Jackson is a great example of a personable leader with strengths such as poise, caring, and an ability to foster trust. His people skills probably weighed heavily in his landing in the final two, especially considering his track record. Kwame was in the boardroom a lot; the men's team lost the first four competitions and even after the teams were reshuffled, he continued to be on losing teams. In fact, he had the dubious distinction of being on the losing team ten out of twelve times! Something was protecting him—his outgoing personality certainly had a great deal to do with it. Those people skills serve him well, and as you will see, he was and continues to be highly sought after since the final episode aired.

Kwame was born in Washington, D.C., but he grew up in Charlotte, North Carolina, and that will always be home. His mother, Marilyn, has always been his inspiration. She was the first person in the family to attend college, earning a scholarship to Howard University, then became a CPA with her own practice in Charlotte. Her success as a businesswoman is a true example of personal and professional determination. Sadly, Kwame's mother died of cancer at just forty-one years old, when Kwame was just fifteen. He has a thoughtful perspective on his mother, who passed along to him her love of knowledge and instilled a sense of poise, dignity, and culture.

A serious but well-liked student, Kwame always knew he was college bound. He earned his B.S. in business administration from

Kwame Jackson, from season one, is a great example of a personable leader.

the University of North Carolina at Chapel Hill, and followed up with an MBA from Harvard University. As an entrepreneurial graduate student in the late 1990s, he was involved in a few dot-com start-ups, but went into sales and marketing at Procter and Gamble after graduation. To appear on the first season of *The Apprentice*, he left his secure position as an investment manager for the prestigious firm of Goldman Sachs. In the end, Donald Trump praised Kwame because his "management training and calm, collected manner separated him from the pack."

Someone with as much infectious appeal and personality as Kwame Jackson would have a hard time confining himself to Wall Street, but at the time of the interview, he was simply curious to see where the opportunity would take him. During casting, no one could argue the fact that he had the perfect credentials for the show; but more than that, he had a delightful way of relating to people that made everyone want to get to know him.

It was interesting to see, as the show developed, how much personality had to do with the contestants' leadership success, and how poor social skills can penetrate the veneer of training and credentials when you put the candidates under stress. It probably wasn't a surprise to the show's creator, Mark Burnett, but it was interesting to test the importance of sociability in a heated and competitive business milieu. *The Apprentice* was a natural laboratory to test the relative importance of technical skills, professional degrees, and character traits in relation to executive-level positions. The first person to be fired was the most credentialed. Kwame, the runner-up in the credential department, was not only well educated but also had an affable, outgoing nature and easily bonded with all of the other candidates. Even though he found himself in a cutthroat environ-

> *The Apprentice* was a natural laboratory to test the relative importance of technical skills, professional degrees, and character traits in relation to executive-level positions.

ment, Kwame found a way to swim in the shark-filled waters of a fierce thirteen-week job interview without damaging his relationships with people.

Kwame created an environment of trust, which is vital in today's corporate environment. Since 1985, nearly 20 percent of America's workforce has been laid off at least once, making the bond between the organization and its people tenuous, at best. So it is more important than ever that the emotional bonds offered by a business leader mend the holes in the safety net that organizations used to provide.

> It is more important than ever that the emotional bonds offered by a business leader mend the holes in the safety net that organizations used to provide.

Resonance

People look to their leaders for connection in both social and emotional contexts. If a person is relating to others in the group in a way that is congruent with its emotional tone she is said to be *resonant*. Resonance occurs when two people are on the same emotional wavelength.[9] Social awareness and the desire to build relationships drive a person's ability to tune in to another's emotional needs.

> Resonance occurs when two people are on the same emotional wavelength.

Resonance allows a leader to maximize the potential of each person on a team, based on the individual's sense of values, priorities, and goals. Dissonant leaders plow over everyone to get the job done. They put the pressure on, thinking this will motivate when it really has the opposite effect. They act as if it doesn't matter that others are left angry or bitter. But as we saw earlier, this attitude is likely to bring revenge in some fashion. All other things being equal, the resonant leader typically does better than the dissonant one in the long run.

On a team, all of the energy that would have gone into being disgruntled and thinking up clever ways to sabotage the leader instead gets channeled into the team effort. When team members are tuned in to each other—when the team resonates—it will be a top-performing team.[10]

> **When team members are tuned in to each other—when the team resonates—it will be a top-performing team.**

Friendship in the Boardroom

In another episode, it was Troy McClain's time to be fired, but what stands out about that night is the remarkable friendship he and Kwame had formed. When it was Troy's time to choose whom he would bring back in with him, he wanted to "invite Kwame to the boardroom" to enjoy "the battle we are going to pursue." Kwame's relationship with Troy McClain was probably the strongest bond that has been forged on any season of *The Apprentice*.

Investment guru Charles Schwab has said, "Lead the life that will make you kindly and friendly to everyone about you, and you will be surprised what a happy life you will lead."[11] That is definitely true for Kwame. After contestant Bill Rancic was hired by Donald Trump, Mark Cuban, the billionaire owner of the Dallas Mavericks, waited for hours at Kwame's after-show party so that he could make Kwame a job offer. Kwame's old firm, Goldman Sachs, also offered him a substantial salary. Although he "lost" the apprenticeship, Kwame has become one of reality television's most sought-after public speakers. He addresses both college students and Fortune 500 company executives, the latter including those from American Express, PricewaterhouseCoopers, and General Electric.

Most recently, Kwame was honored as the first African-American guest speaker sponsored by the London School of Economics Students' Union Business Society at the prestigious London School of Economics and Political Science. He has a $3.8 billion real estate deal in the works, a company called Legacy Holdings, and lifetime bragging rights to having survived ten boardrooms in the very first season of a show that will certainly leave an indelible mark on popular culture. Life is coming up roses for Kwame, who is a great example of the idea that treating people decently really does matter.

Shyness and Attachment

What is it that makes someone like Kwame so comfortable around other people? Is it a skill you can learn if you aren't naturally sociable? The tendency to be outgoing and friendly is partially inborn and partially learned, but it is certainly something that can be developed with a little practice. Even as an adult, you can improve your people skills, as you'll learn in "The Guide for Increasing Sociability and Improving Relationships" section at the end of this chapter.

> Investment guru Charles Schwab has said, "Lead the life that will make you kindly and friendly to everyone about you, and you will be surprised what a happy life you will lead."

Shyness is a big problem for some adults. It is interesting that the propensity to be either shy or gregarious is evident even in newborns. As early as the first year of life, individual differences emerge when it comes to how infants react to strangers.[12] Some infants smile and reach out when they see a new face; some don't mind being held and cuddled. Others need a brief warm-up and will periodically check back with Mom, while others get downright distressed.

Shyness is quite likely to show up at a very early age, but it takes adoption studies to really determine whether there is a genetic component to sociability. For instance, when it comes to introversion and extroversion, identical twins resemble each other more closely than do fraternal twins. Despite the strong evidence, genetic influences can be changed. For example, in the case of shy children who are adopted, they can acquire some of their adoptive parents' social skills. Likewise, if parents work with their extremely shy children, the children will become more socially comfortable. Some of the emotional intelligence training for children is quite successful at helping them overcome shyness.

Certain temperaments, especially shyness, are inborn, but the influence that parents have cannot be denied. Regardless of whether they are inborn or fostered in the family, the attachment patterns developed in early childhood remain our old fallback when we encounter new social situations as adults. In the 1960s, an experiment was devised to test the attachment of mother and child in what was called the "Strange Situation."[13] In this experiment, a researcher placed a mother and her child of about one year of age alone in an unfamiliar room with toys. After a few minutes a researcher came to sit in the room and a few minutes later the mother left. What was of most interest was the baby's behavior when the mother returned. The reactions of the children fall into three major categories of attachment: secure, anxious/resistant, and anxious/avoidant.

> Regardless of whether they are inborn or fostered in the family, the attachment patterns developed in early childhood remain our old fallback when we encounter new social situations as adults.

The securely attached child became pretty distressed when Mom left the room but was easily soothed when she returned. After a few minutes the child felt steady enough to play with the toys again. This "secure" style is seen as the most adaptive attachment style.

The anxious/resistant kid seemed a little reluctant to explore even when Mom was in the room, and when she departed, the child got extremely distressed. When Mom reentered the room, however, the child wouldn't allow itself to be soothed. This is a child who wants affection and attachment, but has a hard time trusting and feeling comfortable that others will give it what it needs.

In the third attachment style, anxious/avoidant, the child seemed distant and aloof, avoiding mom when she was there and showing little emotion when she left. This child doesn't let itself get too dependent and it learns to take care of itself emotionally.

Studies that follow these infants to adulthood find that securely attached people have trust in others, are self-confident, and get a great deal of joy and satisfaction from their relationships with others. On the other hand, people with insecure attachments struggle in life, can find relationships to be a source of conflict, and can be either uncomfortable with closeness (anxious/avoidant) or sensitive and clingy (anxious/resistant).

Fortunately, attachment styles can be changed. There are some exercises in the last section of this chapter that will help you improve your attachment style so you may be more content with both intimate and casual relationships. In fact, I often hear tales of dramatic changes in people's interpersonal styles. There are plenty of people who are outgoing and gregarious who as children often had troubled relationships with their families and peers. Something later in life made them determined to break out of that pattern.

On the surface, being shy seems to result from inheriting the personality traits of shyness and then having adult figures in your early life impact what your future relationships will look like. Although this dynamic undoubtedly occurs, there are always the exceptions to the rule. Judging from the stories of remarkable and "super-normal" people who score high on optimism, extroversion, and resilience tests, there are those who were born with an abundance of these positive qualities and they can withstand a great deal that life throws their way. There are others who aren't so genetically blessed, but there is a kernel of strength waiting inside, and with very little prompting, these people truly blossom. There is hope no matter where you are on the interpersonal continuum—there is always room for improvement. If you like being an introvert, there is good reason to push yourself out of your comfort zone because, in the world of leadership, there is a demand for people to be outgoing.

The Extrovert Advantage

Our culture, especially the business world, favors the extrovert. There are plenty of jobs for introverted people in engineering, information technology, and science, but even in those fields, some of the more high-tech positions have lower status because technicians generally are left out of the strategic planning that defines the objectives of a corporation. Even within the high-tech arena, someone with technical skills has to pass the information along to the rest of us, creating jobs where people skills are crucial, like engineering sales or computer consulting. Even if you are content to sit in the back room and crunch numbers or analyze software, you can end up feeling ignored and undervalued because you aren't part of the decision-making team.

> Our culture, especially the business world, favors the extrovert. There are plenty of jobs for introverted people in engineering, information technology, and science, but even in those fields, some of the more high-tech positions have lower status.

Aside from being in the loop, there are other advantages to being sociable. For example, people who are introverted and more reserved by nature may have fantastic ideas brewing, but they typically take longer to think the thoughts through and share them with others. Because extroverts draw energy from those around them and love to talk, they are more expressive and therefore get more of their ideas on the table. Being an extrovert also has the advantage of creating a buzz and making sure you are remembered when it comes to new ventures. It helps to keep people involved in the corporate politics and decision making instead of feeling ignored and undervalued.

Many of *The Apprentice* contestants say that they get a little disoriented when they join the rest of the cast because they are used to being the loud, talkative member of the team and suddenly they find themselves with even more extroverted people. They often say that they are quieter than they have ever been before—because someone in the group has to listen! Perhaps this sounds self-absorbed, and I confess that when I first started this job, I thought the same thing. I have, however, revised my thinking about extroverts since I have observed their ability to liven a group and get people motivated.

Although I was hired to help the contestants through the reality-show process, I don't know who has gotten more out of the experience, and I suspect sometimes that I have ended up with the better end of the deal. As I have watched these high-energy extroverts go through the disappointments, I have come to realize that what looks like self-absorption is really healthy social interest. When extroverts are disappointed, they turn outward to other people, and that is what helps them stay upbeat and happy. They don't want to stay in their rooms and mull it over; they want to get out with other people and talk about it. I now have to question if it isn't really the introvert who is more self-absorbed.

The extrovert draws people into the process at hand. They are always relating to other people and thinking things over as they go along, involving other people on the way. This is also the very essence of teamwork. And extroversion is a great quality to have as a leader. The leader who focuses on paperwork and e-mail doesn't build morale and involve the team in reaching the goal. The extrovert leader is able to spread enthusiasm to the team. Indeed, relating to people with excitement and passion creates excitement and passion in those other people.

> The extrovert draws people into the process at hand. They are always relating to other people and thinking things over as they go along, involving other people on the way.

Granted, there are degrees of extroversion and many points on the continuum. Most people are not a pure example of introversion or extroversion, although *The Apprentice* candidates definitely are at the far end of the scale. Of course, there is time to listen and time to take center stage, and a raving extrovert who is insensitive to others will not make a good leader. But in general, social interest and friendliness are valuable commodities in the business world because they help foster group cohesion.

Indeed, the extroverted leader is able to work out ideas out with the group; this keeps everyone's spirits up during times of stress. Instead of everyone's retreating to his corner to lick his wounds as a way of dealing with disappointment, the extrovert leader encourages members to stay focused on each other and work things out in the group. This keeps up the momentum of excitement and enthusiasm, even when there are problems. It is part of that upward spiral of optimism and sociability.

> A raving extrovert who is insensitive to others will not make a good leader. But in general, social interest and friendliness are valuable commodities in the business world because they help foster group cohesion.

Seeing People Through Rose-Colored Glasses

It is interesting to listen to an extrovert's perspective on people. Extroverts tend to look at people with a "glass-half-full" perspective. As was mentioned in Chapter 2, family histories are given in a much more positive light. One of the more outgoing contestants on *The Apprentice* explained that his father was blustery, critical, and rarely affectionate, but "that was just his way of expressing love." These extroverts give people the benefit of the doubt; their sociability makes them overlook any faults they might find with someone.

Although marriages are different from work relationships, some of the research that has come out about marriage applies to our general ability to socialize and suggests that there is a powerful connection between optimism and relatedness. Why is it that some days, when someone you know leaves the cap off the toothpaste or leaves the newspaper piled on the table (you know who I'm talking about), it seems kind of cute, while other days it's a personal and malicious attack? It's possible that some days your roommate really is up to no good, but a more likely explanation is that you are looking at the offense without your rose-colored glasses.

As was previously mentioned, satisfied, optimistic couples see virtues in their partners that other people don't see, and they focus on the strengths of the relationship rather than the weaknesses.[14] On the flip side, couples who are dissatisfied and ready to throw in the towel view their partners' intentions in the darkest terms. An innocent glance can be construed as a look of contempt or criticism. The same holds true for social relationships in the workplace. Interpreting your co-worker's slow style to some malicious attempt to annoy you is not the outlook that fosters a healthy work relationship.

Marriage experts can predict with 94 percent accuracy which couples will end in divorce.[15] The same negative habits that ruin a marriage also destroy relationships at work. Here are some of the things that doom a relationship:

- Criticism rather than constructive complaints

- Harboring contempt

- Defensiveness

- Disagreements that quickly escalate

- Failure to validate the other person

- Stonewalling

- Negative nonverbal communication

Optimism is the foundation of good leadership, and this is one of the great contributions of an extrovert leader. Seeing the best in people will bring out their best. If you stew on their shortcomings, not only do you waste energy that could be used for something else, you're also more likely to have difficulty relating with that person, which can affect the whole team. Putting a stop to the habit of criticizing and giving negative interpretations involves reevaluating your explanations of others' behavior.

Criticism figures prominently in difficult and sometimes hostile relationships. If you're prone to criticize, you're not alone; it's an easy trap to fall into. Why is it such a common stumbling block in relationships? How can you transform into a person who's more optimistic and less critical of other people's shortcomings? You'll find suggestions in "The Guide for Increasing Sociability and Improving Relationships" at the end of this chapter that will enhance your sociability through changing critical and negative thinking patterns about other people.

> Optimism is the foundation of good leadership, and this is one of the great contributions of an extrovert leader. Seeing the best in people will bring out their best.

Shed a Little Light on Your Shadow

Sometimes, try as you might, even revising your attitudes can't change the way you feel. Criticism can wear disguises, but they're pretty easy to spot, in both personal and casual relationships. For example, if you often find fault with others, that fault may really be something you secretly wish you had more of yourself. Say you're appalled when a woman in your office is loud and speaks out of turn in meetings. If you take a deeper look, you may find that you have trouble asserting yourself and that your discomfort is really more about what you lack than what she has in spades.

We all have parts of ourselves that are undeveloped and largely unknown. For instance, if you are always extremely polite, you may have trouble expressing anger; if you are habitually explosive, you may have trouble being tender and vulnerable. There are bits of our personality that we are unaware of or are afraid of. Those very traits can catch us off guard when we run into them in others, which makes it difficult to relate and be sociable. So, finding the source of your reaction to someone else will give you insight into yourself. After all, it's in our social relationships that we learn important information about ourselves.

In the next section, you'll find specific suggestions for increasing your sociability and improving the quality of your relationships, and these suggestions will work for both close, intimate relationships and casual, even impersonal ones.

The Guide for Increasing Sociability and Improving Relationships

Initial Steps

Make a list of what bothers you most about someone who is irritating you. It could be someone close to you, such as a spouse or close friend, or it could be an employee or co-worker. Then go over the list in these ways:

1. Edit the list, watching out for "all or nothing" or "black and white" statements.

    Examples:

    "He/she never gets anything done." (all or nothing)

    "She/he is always a selfish person." (black and white)

2. Rewrite the statement to reflect a more realistic approach wherever you find one of these "cognitive distortions."

    Examples:

    "She doesn't get things done when she has more than one task to complete."

    "He is selfish about picking the best projects for himself."

3. Argue with yourself over each item on the list by writing down answers to the following. (For illustration, I show a possible response to an item that says "He is dragging his feet on this project just to get back at me.")

What is the evidence? ("He is probably mad because I gave him a bad evaluation last year.")

Are there any alternative explanations? ("He's been really preoccupied with a new client he just received.")

If this is true, what is the worst that could happen? ("It won't get done and it will reflect badly on me.")

What is the effect of the thought? (For example, "It makes me angry," or sad, or happy, or will probably lead to an argument.)

What could I do about it? ("Talk to him and find out if he is still harboring some feelings about the evaluation. Let him know how much he has improved since then.")

What would I tell a friend who faced this same problem? ("I would tell her she can only do her best to improve the working relationship but the other person has to be willing to try too.")

4. Search the list for criticisms. See if you can trace it to a bad habit of pessimistic thinking.

   Example:

   "He is doing this to get back at me, this always happens, and it will never get any better." (Write an explanation—a nonpersonal, specific, and temporary explanation for what happened.)

Once you've come up with an edited list, set aside time when you and your co-worker are both relaxed and receptive, and talk about what's bothering you. Be specific in talking about the problem and what needs to change. In holding this conversation, keep these points in mind:

- **Be clear in your request**. "I want you to work faster" is not as helpful as "I would like you to let me know early on if you are having trouble with getting a project finished by the due date."

- **Be mindful of nonverbal communication**. If this has been bothering you for a long time, there could be resentment that you may or may not be aware of. In order to decrease the defensiveness of the person you are speaking to, be mindful of hints you may give about your irritation. This includes tone of voice, posture, eye contact, and the distance you keep.

Further Steps

Tips for Overcoming Shyness

- Focus on your interest in other people. Ask them questions to help you get to know them and concentrate on their answers so that you can talk about it later. Being genuinely interested in others makes other people feel interesting!

- Fake it! Hold your head high, stand tall, and make eye contact.

- Watch a friend who is social and extroverted. Watch how he handles himself in social situations.

- When you think about an upcoming event, imagine what the event will be like and what will interest you most, instead of how nervous you might be socializing.

- If you experience uncomfortable levels of anxiety when you think about a social event, consider consulting a cognitive behavioral therapist who specializes in social anxiety. She will be able to help you, often in very few sessions, with relaxation techniques and visualizations that are quite effective at alleviating social anxiety (as well as other phobias).

- You can practice the following technique on your own for overcoming social fears. On a piece of paper, list the order of events that would occur in a social setting. For example, the following might apply for going to an office party: receive an invitation; call to RSVP; get ready for the party; get in the car; walk to the front door where the party is; open the door; start a conversation with one of the guests. After you have your list, vividly imagine each situation—picture every detail, such as who will be at the party and where you will stand. After you have a clear picture (start with the first in the chain of events) take deep breaths and think the word "relax" while releasing any tension you notice in your muscles. Practice this several times for each item on the list. Once you practice relaxing, it will be easier to manage your anxiety on the day of the event.

The following books may also be helpful in alleviating shyness:

- *Overcoming Shyness and Social Phobia: A Step-by Step Guide* by Ronald M. Rapee (Northvale, N.J.: Jason Aronson, 1998)

- *Overcoming Shyness* by M. Blaine Smith (Downers Grove, Ill.: InterVarsity Press, 1993)

- *The Anxiety and Phobia Workbook, 3rd Edition*, by Edmund J. Bourne, Ph.D. (Oakland, Calif.: New Harbinger Publications, 2000)

- *Mind Over Mood: Change How You Feel By Changing the Way You Think* by Dennis Greenberger and Christine A. Padesky (New York: The Guilford Press, 1996)

Going Beyond

- **Search the list you made in "Initial Steps" again for any of your own "shadows."** Remember that the shadows are those undeveloped parts of yourself that you are uncomfortable with. If you find one of those undeveloped parts of yourself, identify what you need to create more balance. Do you need to be more assertive, spontaneous, friendly, or sensitive?

- **List the other person's strengths**. Remember the power of optimism to transform your outlook. A focus on strengths can correct a negative viewpoint. Strengths on this list can include items such as:

  Curiosity

  Love of learning

  Integrity

  Sense of humor

  Kindness

  Fairness

- **Write a paragraph about each of the three strengths that are most important to you**. Include a specific time you saw that strength in that person. Spend some time each day focusing on these strengths.

- **Practice some of the things that help build a successful relationship** (this works quite well at home too!):

  Be curious and find out what the other person is going to do that day or during a weekend.

  Say "Hello" every morning and say "Goodbye" at the end of the day.

  At the end of the workday, have a low-stress conversation.

  Show consideration—smile, make eye contact, and ask questions.

  Express genuine appreciation on a regular basis.

A moment of eye contact with a stranger can make a world of difference; acknowledging another person can leave you with a sense of connection to the human society surrounding you.

Remember, the people who make it through the rigorous selection process for a reality show don't get chosen just because of their business ability, college degree, or good looks. Almost uniformly, they are interesting because they are genuinely sociable and outgoing. It's likely that their optimism in life comes at least in part from their connectedness. When you can be socially comfortable and bond even with strangers, you begin an upward spiral of health, well-being, and success.

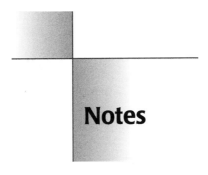

Notes

Chapter One

1. Fredrickson, B. L. (2001). The role of positive emotions in positive psychology: The broaden-and-build theory of positive emotions. *American Psychologist, 56*, 218–226.

2. Seligman, M. E. P. (2002). *Authentic happiness* (p. 134). New York: Free Press.

3. Seligman, M. E. P. (1990). *Learned optimism* (p. 7). New York: Pocket Books.

4. Ibid, p. 9.

5. Greenberg, L. S. (2002). *Emotion-focused therapy* (p. 193). Washington, D.C.: American Psychological Association.

6. http://www.wic.org/bio/roosevel.htm

7. http://www.jbemmons.com/reallives.htm

8. Pooley, E. (2001). *Time*: 2001 person of the year, mayor of the world. Retrieved June 8, 2004, from TIME Online, http://www.time.com/time/poy2001/poyprofile.html

9. Ibid.

10. Ibid.

11. Giuliani: Relentless preparation is the key. Retrieved from News from HIMSS on November 12, 2005, http://www.health datamanagement.com/html/supplements/himss2003/HIMSS NewsStory

12. Smitten, R. (2001). *Jesse Livermore, The world's greatest stock trader.* New York: John Wiley.

13. Gerstner, L.V. (2002). *Who says elephants can't dance?.* New York: HarperCollins.

Chapter Two

1. Seligman, M. E. P. (2002). *Authentic happiness* (p. 39). New York: Free Press.

2. Ibid (p. 24).

3. Ibid (p. 39).

4. Bain, G. H., Lemmon, H., Teunisse, S., Starr, J., Fox, H., Deary, I. J., & Whalley, L. J. (2003). Quality of life in healthy old age: Relationships with childhood IQ, minor psychological symptoms and optimism. *Social Psychiatry and Psychiatric Epidimiology, 38*(11), 632–636.

5. Gibson, B., & Sanbonmatsu, D.M. (2004). Optimism, pessimism, and gambling: The downside of optimism. *Personality & Social Psychology Bulletin, 30*(2), 149–160.

6. Miller, A. (1998). *Death of a salesman.* New York: Penguin Books.

7. Schulman, P., (1999). Applying learned optimism to increase sales productivity. *Journal of Personal Selling and Sales Management, 19*(1), 31–37.

8. Seligman, M. E. P. (1990). *Learned optimism* (pp. 97–103). New York: Pocket Books.

9. Trump, D. J., & Schwartz, T. (1987). *Trump: The art of the deal* (p. 43). New York: Random House.

10. Bennis, W. (1999). The leadership advantage. Leader to leader, 12. Retrieved June 8, 2004, from Leader to Leader Institute, http://leadertoleader.org/leaderbooks/l2l/spring99/ bennis.html

11. Ibid.

12. Maslow, A. H., Stephens, D. C., & Heil, G. (1998). *Maslow on management*. New York: John Wiley.

13. Kim, J., Nicassio, P., Radojevic, V., & Siegel, L. (1995). *The interrelationship among stress, pain, and depression in fibromyalgia.* Paper presented at the annual meeting of the Association of Rheumatology Health Professionals, San Francisco, CA.

14. Seligman, *Learned Optimism*, pp. 43–52.

15. Yu, C. L. M., Fielding, R., & Chan, C. L. W. (2003). The mediating role of optimism on post-radiation quality of life in nasopharyngeal carcinoma. *Quality of Life Research: An International Journal of Quality of Life Aspects of Treatment, Care & Rehabilitation, 12*(1), 41–51.

16. Kubzansky, L. D., Wright, R. J., Cohen, S., Weiss, S., Rosner, B., & Sparrow, D. (2002). Breathing easy: A prospective study of optimism and pulmonary function in the normative aging study. *Annals of Behavioral Medicine, 24*(4), 345–353.

17. Benton, D. A. (2003). *Executive charisma* (p. 131). New York: McGraw-Hill.

18. Lyubomirsky, S., & Lepper, H. S. (1999). A measure of subjective happiness: Preliminary reliability and construct validation. *Social Indicators Research, 46*, 137–155. With kind permission of Sonja Lyubomirsky and Springer Press.

Chapter Three

1. Elliot, J. The power and pathology of prejudice. In Zimbardo, P. G., & Ruch, F. L. (1977). *Psychology and Life*, 9th ed. Glenview, Ill.: Scott Foresman.

2. Seligman, M. E. P. (2002). *Authentic happiness* (p. 37). New York: Free Press.

3. Grawitch, M. J., Munz, D. C., & Kramer, T. J. (2003). Effects of member mood states on creative performance in temporary workgroups. *Group Dynamics: Theory, Research, and Practice, 7*(1), 41–54.

4. Siegel, B. S. (1989). *Peace, love, and healing: Bodymind communication & the path to self-healing: An exploration* (p. 286). New York: HarperPerennial.

5. Burnett, M. (2005). *Jump in!* (p. 26). New York: Ballantine.

6. Csikszentmihalyi, M. (1997). *Finding flow: The psychology of engagement with everyday life*. New York: Basic Books.

7. Seligman, *Authentic happiness*, p. 37.

8. Csikszentmihalyi, *Finding flow*, p. 21.

9. Ibid, p. 100.

10. Moore's law made real by innovation. Retrieved from Intel Technology and Research on September 10, 2004, http://www.intel.com/technology/silicon/mooreslaw

11. A brief history of the minivan. Retrieved from allpar.com on September 10, 2004, http://www.allpar.com/model/m/history.html

12. Hesselbein, F. (2001). When the roll is called in 2010. Leader to Leader, 20. Retrieved September 10, 2004, from Leader to Leader Institute, http://leadertoleader.org/leaderbooks/l2l/spring2001/fh.html

13. http://www.3m.com

14. Hesselbein, When the roll is called in 2010.

15. Trump, D. J., & Schwartz, T. (1987). *Trump: The art of the deal* (p. 3). New York: Random House.

16. Maslow, A. H., Stephens, D. C., & Heil, G. (1998). *Maslow on management* (p. 13). New York: John Wiley.

17. Ibid.

18. Hesselbein, When the roll is called in 2010.

19. Benton, D. A. (2003). *Executive charisma* (p. 17). New York: McGraw-Hill.

20. Goldberg, N. (1986). *Writing down the bones: Freeing the writer within*. Boston & London: Shambhala.

21. Cameron, J. (1992). *The artist's way: A spiritual path to higher creativity*. New York: G.P. Putnam's Sons.

Chapter Four

1. Kelly, C. S. (1997, January 27). Steve Jobs envisions a rhapsody in yellow for Apple's comeback. Retrieved on September 10, 2004, from Government Computer News. http://www.gcn.com/16_2/news/32023-1.html

2. Masten, A. S. (2001). Ordinary magic: Resilience processes in development. *American Psychologist, 56,* 227–238.

3. Bonanno, G. A. (2004). Loss, trauma, and human resilience: Have we underestimated the human capacity to thrive after extremely aversive events? *American Psychologist, 59,* 20–28.

4. Frederickson, B. L., Tugade, M. M., Waugh, C. E., & Larkin, G. R. (2003). What good are positive emotions in crisis? A prospective study of resilience and emotions following the terrorist attacks on the United States on September 11th, 2001. *Journal of Personality and Social Psychology, 84,* 365–376.

5. Siebert, A. (1996*). The survivor personality: Why some people are stronger, smarter, and more skillful at handling life's difficulties . . . and how you can be, too* (Rev. ed.) (p. 243). New York: Berkley Publishing Group.

6. Seligman, M. E. P. (1990). *Learned optimism* (pp. 22–28). New York: Pocket Books.

7. Seligman, M. E. P. (2002). *Authentic happiness* (p. 23). New York: Free Press.

8. Angle, R., & Neimark, J. (1997, July/August). Nature's clone. Retrieved from *Psychology Today* on September 12, 2004, http://www.psychologytoday.com/articles/pto-19970701-000040.html

9. Ibid.

10. Siebert, *The survivor personality.*

11. Brinkman, R., & Kirschner, R. (2003). *Dealing with people you can't stand.* New York: McGraw-Hill.

12. Sotnac, E. (1998). Aikido primer. Retrieved on October 27, 2004, from http://www.aiki.co.yu/primer.htm

13. Fine, M. A., & Schwebel, A. I. (1991). Resiliency in black children from single-parent families. In W. A. Rhodes & W. K. Brown (Eds.), *Why some children succeed despite the odds* (pp. 23–40). New York: Praeger.

14. Siebert, *The survivor personality*, p. 35.

15. Benton, D.A. (2003). *Executive charisma* (p. 131). New York: McGraw-Hill.

Chapter Five

1. Shoda, Y., Mischel, W., & Peake, P. K. (1990). Predicting adolescent cognitive and self-regulatory competencies from preschool delay of gratification. *Developmental Psychology, 26*(6), 978–986.

2. Rancic, B. (2004). *You're hired* (p. 2). New York: HarperCollins.

3. Benton, D. A. (2003). *Executive charisma* (p. 64). New York: McGraw-Hill.

4. Ibid, pp. 61–62.

5. Pence, C. (2004, August 27). Local enters the boardroom. Retrieved on November 3, 2004, from Vail Daily, http://www.vaildaily.com/apps/pbcs.dll/article?AID=/20040827/AE/108270006/-1/VAILNET

6. Turner, R. (2003, November 23). Executive life: In learning hurdles, lessons for success. *New York Times*, p. C-10.

7. Ibid.

8. Hallowell, E., & Ratey, J. (1994). *Driven to distraction*. New York: Pantheon Books.

9. Ibid.

10. Maslow, A. H., Stephens, D. C., & Heil, G. (1998). *Maslow on Management* (p. 14). New York: John Wiley.

11. Trump, D. J., & Bohner, K. (1997). *The art of the comeback* (p. 5). New York: Random House.

12. Ibid, p. 198.

Chapter Six

1. Greenberg, L. S. (2002). *Emotion-focused therapy: Coaching clients to work through their feelings* (p. 4). Washington, D.C.: American Psychological Association.

2. Sorce, J. F., Emde, R. N., Campos, J. J., & Klinnert, M. D. (1985). Maternal emotional signaling: Its effect on the visual cliff behavior of 1-year olds. *Developmental Psychology*, *21*(1), 195–200.

3. Goleman, D. (1995). *Emotional intelligence: Why it can matter more than IQ*. New York: Bantam Books.

4. Thottam, J. (2005, January 17). The science of happiness, Thank God it's Monday. *Time*, p. A59.

5. Mayer, J. D., Caurso, D. R., & Salovey, P. (2000). Emotional intelligence meets traditional standards for an intelligence. *Intelligence*, *27*(4), 267–298

6. Prescosolido, A. T. (2002). Emergent leaders as managers of group emotion. *Leadership Quarterly*, *13*(5), 583–599.

7. Goleman, D., Boyatzis, R., & McKee, A. (2002). *Primal leadership: Realizing the power of emotional intelligence* (p. 19). Boston, MA: Harvard Business School Press.

8. Maslow, A. H., Stephens, D. C., & Heil, G. (1998). *Maslow on Management*. New York: John Wiley.

9. Goleman, D. (1995). *Emotional intelligence: Why it can matter more than IQ* (p. 47). New York: Bantam Books.

10. http://www.quotationspage.com/quote/3105.html

11. Chang, P. P., Ford, D. E., Meoni, L. A., Wang, N. Y., & Klag, M. J. (2002, April). Anger in young men and subsequent premature cardiovascular disease: The precursors study. *Archives of Internal Medicine, 162*, 901–906.

12. Kennedy-Moore, E., & Watson, J. C. (1999). *Expressing emotion: Myths, realities, and therapeutic strategies*. New York: Guilford Press.

13. Seligman, M. E. P. (1990). *Learned optimism* (p. 75). New York: Pocket Books.

14. Goleman, *Emotional intelligence*, p. 308.

15. Siegel, D. J. (1999). *The developing mind: Toward a neurobiology of interpersonal experience* (p. 121). New York: Guilford Press.

16. Mehrabian, A. (1972). *Nonverbal communication*. Chicago, IL: Aldine-Atherton.

17. Kindlon, D., & Thompson, M. (1999). *Raising cain: Protecting the emotional life of boys*. New York: Ballantine Books.

18. Ibid, p. 11.

19. Ibid, p. xix.

20. Goleman, *Emotional intelligence*, p. 153.

21. Goleman, Boyatzis, & McKee, *Primal leadership*, p. 153.

22. Ibid, p. 55.

Chapter Seven

1. Aspinwall, L. G., & Staudinger, U. M. (eds.). (2003). *A psychology of human strengths: Fundamental questions*

and future directions for a positive psychology (p. 41). Washington, D.C.: American Psychological Association.

2. Aspinwall, & Staudinger, *A psychology of human strengths*, p. 42.

3. Adler, A. (1979). Ansbacher, H. L. & Ansbacher, R. R. (eds.). *Superiority and social interest: a collection of later writings*, 3rd rev. ed. (p. 7). New York: Norton.

4. Seligman, M. E. P. (2002). *Authentic happiness* (p. 187). New York: Free Press.

5. Jowett, S., & Chaundy, V. (2004, December). An investigation into the impact of coach leadership and coach-athlete relationship on group cohesion. *Group Dynamics: Theory, Research, and Practice, 8*(4), 302–311.

6. Skipton, L. (2003). Leadership development for the postindustrial, postmodern information age. *Consulting Psychological Journal: Practice & Research, 55*(1), 3–14.

7. Townsend, J., Phillips, J. S., & Elkins, T. J. (2000, October). Employee retaliation: The neglected consequence of poor leader-member exchange relations. *Journal of Occupational Health Psychology, 5*(4), 457–463.

8. Goleman, D., Boyatzis, R., & McKee, A. (2002). *Primal leadership: Realizing the power of emotional intelligence* (p. 64). Boston: Harvard Business School Press.

9. Ibid, p. 20.

10. Goleman, D. (2002). Leading resonant teams. *Leader to Leader, 25*, 24–30.

11. http://www.qotd.org/archive/2005/02/18.html

12. Daniels, D., & Plomin, R. (1985, January). Origins of individual differences in infant shyness. *Developmental Psychology, 21*(1), 118–121.

13. Bowlby, J. (1969, 1973). *Attachment and loss*, 2 vols. New York: Basic Books.

14. Seligman, M. E. P. (2002). *Authentic happiness* (p. 201). New York: Free Press.

15. Gottman, J. (1994). *Why marriages succeed or fail: and how you can make yours last* (p. 20). New York: Simon & Schuster.

Index

About the Author

LIZA SIEGEL, Ph.D., is a clinical psychologist who is a consulting psychologist for several reality television shows, including *Survivor* and *The Apprentice*. In over fifteen seasons of working in the medium, she has not only been involved with screening, testing, and interviewing of applicants, but has in addition been the person whom the cast-out contestants turn to for help in adjusting.

As an undergraduate in psychology at Northern Kentucky University, Liza learned firsthand the importance of hope and the belief that anything is possible, attending college as a single parent while working several part-time jobs and caring for her young daughter.

She graduated with honors and applied to the U.S. Air Force Officer Training School and served as a Captain during the Gulf War. As an executive officer in the administrative branch of the U.S. Air Force she personally observed and learned the qualities of effective leadership.

Liza earned her Ph.D. from the California School of Professional Psychology in 1998. She taught psychology courses at Antioch Graduate School in Santa Barbara, California, The University of LaVerne in Oxnard, California, and Embry-Riddle Aeronautical University in Oxnard. In addition to teaching and private practice, Liza has made contributions to the area of forensic psychology, publishing a work in 2000 in the *Journal of Forensic Sciences* on offenders with "stalking" behavior; serving as a forensic fellow at the San Diego County Jail; and earning an award from "Forensis" in 2000 for her research in forensics.

Liza lives with her husband in Berkeley, California.

For more information go to www.suitesuccessthebook.com.